boomerang!

boomerang!

COACH YOUR TEAM TO BE THE BEST AND SEE CUSTOMERS COME BACK TIME AFTER TIME!

NICK DRAKE-KNIGHT

ꟼ

PIP
POLLINGER IN PRINT

Pollinger Limited
9 Staple Inn
Holborn
LONDON
WC1V 7QH

www.pollingerltd.com

First published by Pollinger in Print 2007

Cover image by permission of iStock

The moral right of the author has been asserted

A CIP catalogue record is available from the British Library

ISBN 978-1-905665-51-8

Designed and set by seagulls.net

Printed and bound in Great Briatin by Lightning Source

Dedicated to Laird Macfarlane

contents

PART B:
CONTINUE & BEGIN™ WORKSHOP TRANSCRIPT

APPENDIX

ACKNOWLEDGEMENTS

I developed an early version of Continue & Begin™ when lecturing in management and business in the early 1990s. I taught and coached young managers and discovered that by ego strengthening, whilst at the same time challenging the individual to stretch, the student achieved phenomenal shifts in personal performance, built upon a platform of confidence. The origins of the model lay in therapeutic work I was studying at the time.

I used the same approach when working for the DTI funded agency, Business Link. Owners and directors of small and medium sized business owners responded positively when I highlighted the excellence of their achievements and then set about helping them to become 'even better'. It was when my interests shifted to the service sector in 2001 that Continue & Begin™ evolved into its current form. It is a simple to use, and rapid, process that creates phenomenal change in a person's professional life. Continue & Begin™ is equally effective in helping people manage their private affairs. This book, however, remains within the boundaries of work related activity.

Many people have helped me shape what was a fairly crude idea into a coaching approach now used by many of the world's best-known retail, automotive, financial services and public sector organisations. Colleagues, clients, coaches and coachees, even my own family, added value along the way. My son Martin, for example, will be forever known as the 'Structure-of-Well-Done-ness' kid!

Special thanks must go to Fran Osman-Newbury for her critical eye and professionalism, Graeme Taylor and Paul Cooper for the foreword and preface respectively, Marie Shields for simplifying my tortuous syntax, and Joan Deitch at Pollinger for her never-ending encouragement and eternal good humour.

Thank you to all of you.

Nick Drake-Knight
Cliff Cottage, 2007

foreword

Bang & Olufsen is the most highly respected audio, video and communications brand in the world. Our franchisees offer levels of customer service that match the unprecedented focus on quality and finish of all our products.

To ensure the highest possible level of after-sales service, we have certified a number of highly qualified service providers, who provide maintenance and service in accordance with Bang & Olufsen's exacting standards.

Our service providers observe and comply with all technical regulations and guidelines when carrying out maintenance, and continuously attend technical training seminars to maintain and improve their skills, including customer service.

We are dedicated to growing our brand by building financially successful retailers within an exclusive retail environment. In order to do this, the quality of our customer service must match the unparalleled qualities of our products. Our stores engage the customer from the moment they walk in the door by showcasing high-quality design and cutting-edge technology. The service experience must match this product quality.

Like our customers, the service professionals employed by our franchisees come from a variety of backgrounds and have individual personalities. There are, however, certain qualities that all our service professionals share.

A successful customer service professional at Bang & Olufsen will require a level of social presence. That is, the ability to meet and interact with people in a self-assured, but relaxed and friendly manner. Visit our stores and you will find that our service professionals are likely to be self confident, good communicators with the poise and personality required to meet the needs of demanding customers. They'll also be practical, enthusiastic, keen and able to demonstrate the benefits of the Bang & Olufsen brand. And above all, they'll have an overwhelming desire to provide our customers with total service quality.

In order to support our franchisees in meeting the challenging standards we expect, Bang & Olufsen provides extensive training and regular support. A key part of the development process is the coaching of franchisees and their staff in service excellence, to embed their learning and maintain the high standards we (and they) expect. Coaching proficiency is an essential skill for our local store leaders.

What Nick Drake-Knight has done in this book is to explain to professional retailers how they can develop the excellence of their service quality through a culture of coaching. At Bang & Olufsen, we aim for the highest levels of customer service; however, because the benchmark is constantly changing, the challenge for us now is to stay at the top. The Continue & Begin coaching model outlined in this book is a great way of managing that process.

Graeme Taylor
Director of Marketing UK & Benelux
Bang & Olufsen www.bang-olufsen.com

preface

I am delighted to have been asked to provide the preface for this book. The Institute of Customer Service actively supports the growth of service skills in UK business and this book provides an innovative approach to employee learning and development.

Coaching is now recognised as an effective way to accelerate and *sustain* the learning and development of people at work. There is still a place in business for traditional learning methods, although most service professionals accept that, without subsequent reinforcement, the effects of training can be short-lived. Like mud thrown against a wall, most of it slides off. This is especially true of the 'sheep-dip' training in which some organisations indulge – more often driven by the need to tick boxes than to provide deeper understanding for their staff.

Coaching must have a direction. A good customer service coach is one who cares passionately about his or her coachee, and equally passionately about the quality of service experienced by the end-user customer. Truly effective coaches understand the nature of 'excellence' within their industry sectors, whilst recognising the individual development requirements of the people they are coaching. No two people are alike, nor do they learn in quite the same way, or at the same speed. A good coach will see this and tailor the approach accordingly.

A key success factor in people development, and especially where coaching plays a strong role, is to allow time for the individual to embed and apply new learning, and for regular coaching reviews to monitor and encourage progress.

Customer service coaching is not about passing on knowledge, although inevitably the process often results in some degree of knowledge transfer. Coaching is primarily about nurturing the coachee's ability to self-determine, and to achieve maximum performance, to the benefit of the individual, the customer and the employing organisation. A really tough order!

Nowadays, growing great coaches and utilising their skills is tremendously important to business success. Coaching skills can be learnt, and over the past eight years the Institute of Customer Service has trained hundreds of people to become coaches for our ICS Professional Awards programme, many of whom would never have believed they could play such a role. And the best coaches, of course, make the best people to coach other coaches.

The results of great coaching are there for all to see: motivated, professional employees providing great service, and consequently having a major effect on customer satisfaction, customer loyalty and customer retention. Service excellence results in retained customers. Keeping the customers you have is the route to sustained profitability, whilst providing free marketing in the form of referral and advocacy to all those potential *new* customers out there.

This is just as true for the public sector. Replace the word 'profit' with 'service excellence' and the same rules apply.

World-class organisations, either in the public sector or as commercial enterprises, achieve excellence with well-trained and well-*coached* employees.

Paul Cooper
Director, Institute of Customer Service
www.instituteofcustomerservice.com

about the author

Nick Drake-Knight has been a business change consultant and speaker for more than 20 years. In the 1990s, he developed his consulting skills in Europe and the former Soviet Union, before returning to work in the UK as a senior business adviser for the Department of Trade and Industry (DTI)-funded Business Link network. In 2003, Nick advised the DTI on the implementation of revised business support services for SMEs.

NDK Group – the change consultancy firm – has a diverse portfolio of commercial and public-sector clients. NDK Group works for government agencies, the public sector, schools, colleges, and a range of SME clients.

Nick is also a board director of the UK's leading mystery shopping company, Performance in People Ltd, providing advice, guidance and training to many of the UK's (and the world's) top high street, financial services and automotive brands.

He is a professionally qualified clinical hypnotherapist (MBSCH, DHyp) and maintains a small number of private patients. He was trained by NLP co-creator Dr. Richard Bandler to become a Master Practitioner of Neuro-Linguistic

Programming and studied extensively as a student of Dr. John Grinder (co-creator of NLP), with fellow change masters Dr. Frank Farrelly and Dr. Stephen Gilligan, and at the London College of Clinical Hypnosis.

He is an authority on the use of video footage and telephone audio files in coaching and has helped many global brand names to implement his unique Continue & Begin™ coaching model. The model creates behavioural shifts in employees – quickly. Thousands of coaches now use Continue & Begin™.

Nick speaks regularly at national conferences and corporate staff development events. He can be contacted via www.ndk-group.com or by email to nick@ndk-group.com.

In 2004 he co-authored, with Fran Osman-Newbury, *SALES HYPNOSIS: The Structure and Use of Hypnotic Phenomena and Indirect Suggestion in Sales*, 224pp, Hypnotic Business, ISBN 0-9546744-0-5, via www.ndk-group.com.

Nick Drake-Knight lives on the Isle of Wight, off the south coast of Britain. He is married, with four adult children. He is, without doubt, the worst surfer in England.

author's notes

BOOMERANG!
COACH YOUR TEAM TO BE THE BEST
AND SEE CUSTOMERS COME BACK
TIME AFTER TIME!

Service sector businesses, including the retail, automotive, financial services and hospitality industries, are increasingly investing in the 'people skills' of their customer-facing staff. Business leaders recognise that in highly competitive markets, with negligible product differentials, it is the calibre of their people that makes the difference in consumer experience. In the UK alone, in a working population of 29 million, 2.8 million people now work in retail (British Retail Consortium 2007) with an estimated 5.5 million engaged in some form of sales or customer service activity across the country.

In the United States, the figures are much higher. Worldwide, the numbers rise to hundreds of millions of employees.

The people-skills performance of customer-facing employees impacts directly on business profitability. Service skills are a vital component in the customer journey, and yet employers consistently report skills gaps and skills shortages. Customer satisfaction surveys reinforce this message.

Service skills can be taught and employees can be coached to develop their abilities to even higher levels of performance. The businesses that do major on service quality and invest appropriately stand out as leaders in their sectors. Coaching, even more than training, is an essential tool in creating service excellence.

This book explains how a specific type of coaching can be delivered as an everyday part of any manager's job function. Critically, in service sector environments, coaching has to be easy to use and *fast*.

Coaching is massively powerful when combined with visual or telephone mystery shopping. Today, almost all leading retailers make use of mystery shopping as a means of measuring the quality of the customer service experience, including the performances of customer-facing employees.

There are plenty of good coaching models in industry today, but none of them have been developed specifically for a fast-paced retail environment, or to support a mystery shopping programme. This book explains how to use 'observed behaviour', or mystery shopping outputs, in a sensitive and productive coaching session that leaves the coachee feeling more alive than when he or she started! By following this well-proven process, and using carefully crafted language patterns drawn from Neuro-Linguistic Programming (NLP) and other therapeutic disciplines, new coaches learn how to revolutionise staff performance from a platform of *positivity*.

how to use
this book

BOOMERANG! is presented in two parts:

Part A presents the underpinning philosophies and technical models that support Continue & Begin™. Specific linguistic patterns are presented which form the 'tools' of the coaching model. Many of these linguistic tools have their origins in the therapeutic disciplines, adapted for (safe) use in a work context. At the heart of Continue & Begin is ego strengthening and the celebration of existing competences.

Part B of the book is an edited transcript from a training seminar run by Nick Drake-Knight. The seminar, held in 2006, assisted a group of corporate retail, hospitality and automotive business managers in developing their coaching skills, including on-the-spot 'observed behaviour' coaching, and the application of Continue & Begin within a mystery shopping programme.

The training programme narrative, recorded verbatim, supplements the underpinning knowledge contained in Part A. It emphasises that these unique coaching skills can be used with equal effect in day-to-day situations where a manager observes a colleague in action and then coaches him or her on what went well, and how he or she could perform *even better*. It is not necessary to have mystery shopping video footage or telephone audio file recordings to effectively coach someone using the Continue & Begin model.

This book promotes Continue & Begin as a simple and fast-acting coaching methodology that is highly effective on the sales and service floor. It does not critique other established coaching models. Some alternative approaches are highly effective in creating personal change for people; it's just that they tend to be cumbersome and ponderous, and therefore wholly unfit for use in a fast-moving sales or retail environment where speed of application is of the essence.

This book explains how sales and service managers and team leaders can help their people to perform *even better* by themselves becoming *even better* as coaches – quickly!

introduction

Coaching is a hot topic in business. A whole industry is emerging, with 'coaching' having a spectrum of meanings dependant on the sector, the professional discipline, and the seniority of the 'coachee'.

But what is coaching? Isn't it the same as training? Or mentoring? Or is it a bit like counselling?

Let us be clear on this:

Training is a structured, inductive process, sometimes led by a physical trainer, or by other third party instruction (e-learning, online tutorials, hard-copy manuals), and is designed to transfer knowledge, and sometimes skills, to help employees perform specific job tasks. Training helps people learn new skills or new knowledge. Training almost always includes a degree of *telling* on the part of the trainer. Equally, training will sometimes manifest itself in the form of stochastic, trial-and-error experiential learning, where POFO is the norm – Push Off and Find Out. We've all experienced that.

Mentoring provides a 'mentee' with guidance and advice from someone who has experience in a given field, or who has sufficient credibility for the mentee to consider him, or her, worthy of consultation. The mentor may or may not be a line manager. Often mentoring works best when the mentor is an experienced colleague at the same level of seniority, or a more senior colleague who works in a different team, away from the day-to-day environment of the mentee. The mentee is offered advice, or a potential solution or a set of potential solutions, by the mentor.

The merchant navy has a culturally accepted practice of providing a 'Sea Daddy' for new boy sailors. I know because I had a most wonderful Sea Daddy in 1978, when I was a young teenaged apprentice on a deep-sea merchant vessel. I was struggling with being at sea, on the other side of the world, away from my friends and family, and months away from being able to come home. Without my Sea Daddy, Laird, I would have had difficulty coping. He built my confidence, made me feel good, and challenged me to do 'even better'. Many people at work find themselves in need of a Sea Daddy from time to time.

Counselling focuses on personal matters. Counselling is used in therapy. We are not at work to counsel people on issues in their personal lives. That is a job for therapeutic professionals. Managers have a responsibility to recognise when they are at the boundaries of their work roles, and when professional counselling would be helpful for an employee.

Signposting to helpful agencies makes sense – but in my experience of management development, too many managers get into territory that is outside their areas of competence. Delusional beliefs exist that being a boss in some way qualifies you to offer therapeutic interventions. The phenomenal volume of psycho-babble in many of today's management development programmes is, I believe, a worrying trend. There are too many managers (and management development trainers) in business who have convinced themselves that they can 'help' employees in areas way beyond their understanding and capabilities. As the saying goes, "A little bit of knowledge is a dangerous thing." Managers who have recently trained as NLP practitioners take note. Recently trained 'life coaches' take extra note.

Coaching, by contrast, is a process designed to help people identify their own chosen path in relation to a work skill or discipline. It is about *asking*. When work-based coaching is consistently done well, and has become a part of the culture of an organisation, it encourages self-learning, invites creativity and delivers higher performance. It becomes OK for people to 'admit' to work areas in which they need personal development, new skills, or new ways of doing things – when otherwise they might have hidden their uncertainty, or covered up their inadequacies.

When coaching is fully integrated into an organisation, it builds confidence and generates 'response-ability' in individuals; that is, the ability to respond – to take action to improve their ability to perform at work. Ownership by the coachee and self-determination are key facets of effective coaching.

Coaching is about helping people who already have ability and knowledge to further improve their performance – to become *even better*. Primarily it is a process used to stimulate behaviour changes, although changes to thinking patterns are usually an essential precursor to behavioural shifts. Often, the coachee has the answer right in front of him or her. The job of the coach is to help the coachee self-discover a way forward.

Coaching Variants

In Britain alone there are numerous organisations professing to be *the* authority on business coaching, but not a single institute or body exists that can profess to be the acknowledged lead body. A number of self-accredited organisations offer their own versions of certificates or diplomas in coaching. A small number of National Vocational Qualifications are now evolving in the UK that provide the first evidence of a structured approach to work-based coaching. The robustness of the academic content of these programmes varies significantly, with a key variant being the degree to which the impact of language is considered and understood.

The marketplace is crammed full of supposed coaching experts, some of whom have questionable credibility in terms of their competence to deal with the psychological factors involved in helping people to change their thinking and behaviour at work, which, make no mistake, is exactly what coaching is about.

Virtually anyone can describe himself or herself as a 'coach'. The very nature of people is that emotional well-being at work becomes interwoven with domestic life. This creates the potential for poorly trained individuals to operate beyond the boundaries of work-based coaching and, perhaps inadvertently, dabble in psychological matters for which they are ill equipped to operate.

Coaches inevitably touch people's psyches, and this requires a degree of coaching skill that some 'weekend courses' are unlikely to provide. I have witnessed some dreadful examples of managers (and management developers) causing psychological damage to otherwise well-balanced and productive individuals. On too many occasions, clients of mine have described circumstances that can only be described as ham-fisted attempts by a coach to offer 'therapy'. The ego of the coach seems to get in the way of the ego strengthening of the coachee. Bulls in china shops.

My guidance to you is to be wary of all alleged 'coaches', especially 'life coaches'. What qualifies someone to be a coach? Within what parameters?

Coaching as a professional activity requires moderation by an independent professional body or academic institute. Governance is required.

It is with these stark warnings in mind that I commend the Continue & Begin coaching model. The approach is light in terms of psychological impact. In fact, the model proposes ego strengthening as the starting point for change work, with minimal attention given to 'areas for improvement', at least until the coachee has celebrated his or her successes in a given area of operation.

The model is simple in structure, easy to use, and low risk. It requires nothing in the way of 'personal analysis'. It is therefore safe to use, even in the clumsiest of hands.

At a business level, one of the key benefits of Continue & Begin is the speed of application and efficiency of time involvement for both coach and coachee. In retail environments it is essential that any coaching model be quick to use and easy to share with colleagues. Continue & Begin was developed with simplicity in mind. That's why, in just a few years since its inception, so many of today's global brands are now using Continue & Begin to help their people to *continue to* do some things well and to *begin to* do other things differently – maybe *even better* than they already do.

PART A

underpinning principles

1

pits of despair

I've discovered a common pattern of speech when meeting with senior executives of companies I've helped. The executive, usually the operations director of a large retail operator, will set out his or her ambitions for the business. The conversation will go something like this:

> **Ops Director.** We've got a clear business plan for this year. We are in a very competitive marketplace, and our customer satisfaction data is telling us that service quality is the key. In order for us to achieve the goals set out in the plan we have to address *customer experience* as our primary driver for performance improvement.

> **NDK.** I see. What specifically do you have in mind?

> **Ops Director.** We have a challenge with the quality of customer experience in our stores/branches/dealerships. It varies massively. We have some parts of the business that are doing really well in terms of customer experience. The

mystery shopping and customer satisfaction data tell us so. But we also have vast acres of mediocrity where the service quality is just 'OK'. 'OK' simply isn't good enough anymore. And then we have some parts of the business where, frankly, it's a pit of despair. What I want is consistency across the national estate!

After a few years of hearing the same speech each time I visited a national retailer, I began to anticipate the language pattern described above. It's actually quite hard not to say it out loud, as the ops director is about to reveal his or her hidden concerns. If the ops director is struggling to know what he or she wants (a common scenario) I will explain that sometimes when I meet ops directors for the first time they will say to me... and I then describe the above conversation. Time after time, the poor executive nods feverishly and says,

That's exactly what's happening in this business! That's why I want to talk to you about a customer service training programme.

Pockets of excellence, vast acres of mediocrity, and pits of despair exist in every business-to-consumer national or regional operation I've ever worked with. It's a feature of retail networks.

2
the model
of excellence

Here's a question for you: "Is training sufficient to embed new work practices?"

The answer is a definite "No!" and yet, despite this, when it comes to fresh ambitions about customer service quality, staff training is usually in the air. Of course, training plays an important role in service quality improvement. The challenge for senior managers is to choose the most effective training route to create improved skills and new capabilities.

But if we accept that training, on its own, is insufficient to create the changes you want for your business, then how can you ensure that a given approach to learning and development will be effective?

Fortunately, some of the world's leading businesses have a helpful 'success pattern' for training. The pattern (almost!) guarantees consistent, high-octane performance, with that all-important criterion, *sustainability*. The pattern can be used as a guide to developing customer service excellence.

I identified the pattern during years of working with class-leading retail, automotive and financial services operators, and in one or two public sector agencies as well. It seemed that in almost every case, the very best performers in any given business sector had a framework for learning and development that followed a common pattern. The NLP community might call this discovery an output from 'modelling'; I don't think it was anything quite so grand, I just stumbled over it when I had a brief *Eureka!* moment.

The pattern is what Gregory Bateson, the anthropologist and polymath, called a 'pattern which connects'. I call it the Model of Excellence. The model relates to three levels of influence:

1. Explicit standards

World-class operators have an explicit set of performance standards that spell out exactly what is expected of employees. This approach applies irrespective of the discipline, industry sector or activity. Employees need to know what is expected of them if they are to work to a given standard.

This is Level 1 in the Model of Excellence (see diagram).

The ambition of most organisations is that the application of skills and techniques will achieve a performance equal to, or surpassing, the explicit standards. Given the right skills, tools and personal characteristics, this is an effective approach that works well for most employees.

What happens, typically, is that some form of training is provided in an attempt to transfer understanding and to develop the necessary skill sets. Smart operators develop bespoke training solutions that are tailored to suit their precise needs. Off-the-peg training packages rarely embrace the cultural idiosyncrasies of an organisation. Formulaic approaches incur resistance and are sometimes perceived as an imposed regime that the organisation has to 'fit to'.

Even when the training is apparently a perfect match, the experience for many organisations is that, on its own, training has limited impact. In fact, a lot of training goes in one ear and out the other. That's a fact. To make training truly effective it must be memorable.

Class-leading businesses ensure that new knowledge and understanding stays with the trainee long after the session has ended, through a combination of indirect suggestions, metaphors, stories, analogies, fun activities and games, language activities, humour and mild teasing.

Training has to be *fun* and *intriguing* – trainees learn more when they are relaxed and enjoying themselves. If you can make a course delegate or on-the-job trainee curious about learning, they will want more, and more, and more knowledge. And confidence comes from underpinning knowledge. Think about it... when you've been anxious or nervous about a task or activity (maybe a presentation to an influential audience?) it's usually because there's an uncertainty at play; and for many people the uncertainty is caused by gaps in their knowledge about a given topic. All organisations need their people to be confident.

If people enjoy learning, they become confident and are more likely to become *even more* curious about those things they don't know... and then learning becomes a habit. In fact, you might be curious yourself about what you would like to know more about...

2. Consistency

Ask any senior manager in an organisation and he or she will tell you that across his or her national or regional estates there are pockets of performance excellence, vast fields of mediocrity, and occasional pits of despair. Too often, service quality can fluctuate over time between outlets, branches or offices, and this can create real challenges in maintaining a reputation of excellence.

Top-performing organisations strive for consistency of excellence in all geographic and functional areas of their business. Effective training can help with this, especially when it is practically (competence) based and aligned with the explicit standards of performance prescribed by the business.

Buy-in from the top is essential – there's nothing more influential than a senior manager of director participating in some front-line training. After all, culture starts at the top, doesn't it? A degree of 'air cover' helps too. When middle-ranking managers know that they have the backing of the top people to release staff for essential training, it makes attendance on training events easier to justify.

But here's the rub...

Consistency is of limited value if it's temporary. World-class operators know that performance excellence must be delivered day in and day out, long after the latest training initiative has been launched. In some organisations, training is like throwing mud against the wall. Most of the mud slides off the wall immediately.

Consistency is Level 2 in the Model of Excellence.

3. Sustainability

In fact, training is a complete waste of energy and resources unless it is made *sustainable*.

New drives for quality, including the introduction of revised performance standards, are subject to what we refer to as *parachute training*. When organisations implement change, sometimes employees perceive the new project as the 'latest initiative' and the associated training as being delivered by facilitators or consultants who *parachute in*, deliver the training and are then *helicoptered out*. Even the most inspirational training events can be short-lived in terms of longevity of impact.

We've all been on training courses that are informative, good fun and even useful! The challenge for most of us is that when we get back to the day job our early excitement and enthusiasm gradually wanes as the realities of the daily grind take precedence. The commitment to new thinking and behaviour often loses momentum after a period of compliance. Even when the whole team experiences the same learning and development programme – at the same time – the 'stickability' of the training can be questionable. Let's face it: few training activities produce a long-term positive impact on their own.

Not surprising then, that many leading-edge corporations have found this is an ineffective methodology for improving performance.

Key to sustainability (Level 3 of the Model of Excellence) is the development of a coaching philosophy and skill set that allows local managers to keep the plates spinning long after the training event has passed. Sustainability through local coaching and management keeps the momentum up and the training alive!

Training must be supported by local leaders who ensure that trainees get the opportunity, encouragement and coaching to implement their new learning. Otherwise, why were they sent on the course or given the training in the first place?

If you don't currently have a coaching culture and capability embedded within your organisation, get it sorted out! Every professional manager should be able to coach using a consistent methodology – it's a fundamental management competence.

3

implementing the model of excellence

The Model of Excellence is now widely employed across industry sectors and the commercial/public sector divide. Why? Because it creates results.

The starting point, logically, is the creation of an explicit set of standards that people can relate to, that they believe could be achievable, and that they can incorporate into their daily working lives. Too many performance standards are couched in 'management speak' that other colleagues find difficult to digest. Make standards simple, meaningful and relevant and then train colleagues to be able to deliver them.

Of course, they'll need the tools to do the job, and that might mean resource investment. Combine this with a local coaching capability that supports and encourages and you have the building blocks for a sustainable model of working that will create excellence across your organisation.

By creating an internal coaching capability within the organisation, class-leading organisations ensure that excellence is sustained. My guidance to you is to follow in the footsteps of acknowledged class-leaders and apply this Model of Excellence to your operations:

1. Decide on your standards – and make them explicit.

2. Create a coaching culture and coaching skill sets within your organisation.

3. Train your people in the skills they need to succeed at their jobs.

4. Maintain post-training performance outputs through regular coaching by local managers.

4

coaching
for success

A key element of the Model of Excellence is the emphasis on sustaining high standards in service delivery (Level 3). Training provides an opportunity to create service consistency (Level 2) across an organisation, but it is of limited value if employees and managers revert to type and fail to maintain the new order beyond the initial excitement of the training event.

Coaching, facilitated by trained coaching professionals, ensures performance is maintained long after the training session has ended. By developing an internal coaching capability, organisations are able to radically increase the effectiveness of training events and the impact that their new skills have on the end-user customer.

Coaching is a wonderful way to transfer technology to colleagues without having to repeatedly engage trainers from outside the business, with the associated costs, or take staff away from their posts for 'refresher' training.

The most effective approach is to train local team leaders or managers to become coaches. As an on-site, fully trained coach, the local leader has the technical ability and is readily available to conduct regular mini-coaching sessions with his or her colleagues.

5

growing great coaches

Most people have a good understanding of what is required to be a great coach. When I ask any group of wannabe coaches the characteristics of a successful coach, a surprisingly diverse set of attributes and behaviour traits are mentioned:

Attributes of a great coach?

A rapport builder	Passionate
Sympathetic	Honest (about what's relevant)
Supportive	Interested
Empathetic	Inspiring
Encouraging	Enabling
Enthusiastic	Positive
Independent	Suggests options or choice
Objective	Asks about options or choice

Nurturing	Encourages pro's and con's thinking
Challenging	Questions beliefs
A listener	Asks fundamental questions
Questioning	Asks the questions no-one else will
Calm	Future orientated
Thinks contextually	Solution focussed
Knows the boundaries of coaching	Action focussed
Warm hearted	Has a good sense of humour
Gets into the coachee's world	Gains commitment from the coachee
Mildly provocative	Is specific

Quite a specification! Most people have some of these characteristics, and some people have most of them. However, it would seem a tough call to develop all these characteristics in one individual.

Surely, rather than rebuilding a coach's personality, there must be an easier way of building capability? There are at least a few simple generic principles we can work to:

- ● Seeking first to understand

  Understanding the coachee's map of the territory is crucial in developing a personal plan that fits congruently with the requirements of the coachee. We recommend that new coaches seek to understand the professional work goals of their coachees before they embark on the 'change strategy'.

● Asking, not telling

The coach is not there to 'train' or 'instruct' – coaching is more about helping an individual to gain a personal insight into his or her performance at work. It is about giving the coachee some well-deserved space to ask searching questions that he or she can answer for himself or herself.

● Receiving, more than transmitting

My colleagues and I have been training new coaches for many years. The well-trained coach offers objectivity and is as much a listener as a talker. We know that skilled coaches take great care to understand the perspectives of the individuals they work with and the environment within which they are working. Pareto's 80:20 works well in this respect. The coach talks, mostly by contributing observations and asking questions, for 20% of the time, and the coachee responds, often thinking out loud, for 80% of the time.

The coaching principles you will learn in this book are simple and effective – we encourage new coaches to reflect observed behaviour to the coachee and then work with the individual to identify what has worked well for him or her, where opportunities exist to improve even further on performance, and what personal strategies could be put in place to make this happen. The approach you will learn is always supportive and focuses throughout on positives.

Once you have learned the underpinning knowledge contained within this book, and have mastered the delivery of the new skills you will learn, your coachees and their employing organisations will benefit immediately.

Outputs for the coachee will include:

- self-development, learning and growth (for coach as well as coachee!)
- a well thought-through personal action plan
- even greater personal effectiveness
- sharing of new knowledge and personal action plans with colleagues
- subsequent benefits to the employing organisation

Done well, coaching is a productive skill that impacts positively on the psyche of the coachee like no other form of professional development. It requires careful application and is best placed in the hands of competent operatives.

Done poorly, or recklessly, it can cause a huge amount of damage, especially when coaches mistakenly go beyond the boundaries of their abilities and roles. When poor coaching technique is combined with mystery shopping video film, or recorded telephone calls, the impact can be profoundly distressing for the coachee.

It is essential that coaches work to a simple and structured pattern that is easy to use, and effective within the territory of the workplace. The pattern should have clear boundaries on what is in scope, and what lies beyond the coaching role.

6

coaching
application

Coaching can be effectively employed in virtually any work environment. What you will discover in this book is transferable to most organisations, and almost all industry sectors.

The *best fit* for the skills you will learn is in the retail sector, in the broadest definition of 'retail'. Wherever an employee is in communication with customers, the techniques contained in this book will have massive value for the coachee and the customer, and therefore for the employing organisation.

In this book the term 'retail' refers to any business-to-consumer activity where communication takes place directly between a service provider and an end-user customer. This could include traditional high-street retail operations, car dealerships, financial services businesses (and the complexities of regulatory compliance), hospitality businesses, public service providers, and services to customers accessed by telephone, including call centres.

In recent years the coaching model you will learn in this book (Continue & Begin) has been increasingly used in email-based customer communication systems where verbal and non-verbal communication is replaced by the use of the written word, and all the implications that has for accuracy of meaning and effectiveness of two-way communication and understanding.

The model works equally effectively for an internal marketplace within an organisation, where colleagues operate within an internal customer-supplier chain.

This book provides readers with coaching skills in two forms:

1. coaching using 'observed behaviour'

2. coaching using recorded video footage or telephone audio file

The skill sets involved are the same, although the reference points will be different in nature.

7

observed behaviour coaching

'Observed behaviour' relies on both the coach and the coachee having the same perspectives on what has just happened in a given intervention with a customer. Observed behaviour coaching works well when the coach has just watched and listened to an employee in action with a customer, and then coaches him or her on performance. The coach may be a line manager, or perhaps a specialist coaching professional. The same coaching principles apply.

The key to success with observed behaviour coaching is to conduct the coaching session immediately after the coachee has been observed in action, while the experience is fresh in the minds of both coach and coachee. It is very difficult to coach on observed behaviour when the event took place some time previously. Memories fade quickly and there is nothing more challenging in retail coaching than to refer to a customer intervention that happened some hours or even days earlier.

What is great about observed behaviour coaching is how flexible and spontaneous it is. Coaching doesn't have to be some lengthy process requiring detailed planning and personal soul-searching. When coaching is part of the culture of an organisation, some of the best improvement sessions can be achieved off the cuff, in response to an event or activity that has just occurred.

There is nothing more satisfying for a service professional than to be given a few minutes of his or her coach's time to celebrate a service skill that has just been delivered with panache, and to spot an opportunity for future service quality to be equally impressive, and maybe *even better* still!

Observed behaviour coaching has benefits and drawbacks.

Observed behaviour coaching

Benefits	Limitations
Flexible	Differing perspectives of coach and coachee
Immediate	Non-verifiable observations
In situ	Relies on memory
Low cost	

8

mystery shopping coaching

Today many retail operators make use of recorded mystery shopping materials as a means of monitoring and measuring service quality performance. The recordings are available in covertly recorded video format, or on telephone audio files. What businesses do with the secret video recordings and covertly captured telephone calls is the key to success.

If used insensitively, the material can cause emotional and even psychological harm. Get it really wrong and there can be blood on the walls!

When an untrained manager or team leader is let loose with mystery shopping material, the potential for harm that can be caused by his or her 'coaching' is significant. Visual mystery shopping produces a film of an individual or individuals, in action in the work environment, when they are unaware that filming is taking place.

Think about when you have seen yourself on film, maybe from a home video recording or these days even on a mobile phone camera – most people are a little unnerved by what they see and hear! When we combine the feelings of self-consciousness caused by seeing ourselves on film with the inevitable emotions associated with a perceived 'assessment' of our performance at work (when we didn't know it was happening!) there is bound to be a potential for causing psychological harm to the individual featured on film, if the experience is handled carelessly.

Semantic meaning in mystery shopping

When we use words to describe the nature of visual mystery shopping or telephone mystery shopping, it is important to consider the semantic meaning of the words employed.

We can comment on how someone has been:

- caught on film
- captured on film
- featured on film
- recorded on film
- shown on film

We favour the phrase 'featured on film'.

Most people tell us that the word 'featured' has a positive meaning that even has an element of glamour associated with it – a sort of Hollywood actor spin! By contrast, suggesting that someone has been 'caught' has a negative, even quite threatening, meaning. One little word or the syntactic construction of a phrase can radically affect the meaning of our intended communication. Careless use of the English language can create negative, damaging outcomes, even when we mean to be supportive and positive.

Our guidance is to avoid any potential for implying pain and stick to positive messages. People new to visual mystery shopping often have reservations about its intended application and the potential for abuse. They are right to be concerned, as injudicious use can cause great harm. It is essential that an organisation starting out with visual mystery shopping consult with worker representatives and explain the positive, beneficial nature of this wonderful resource, and how it will be used to develop the skill sets of colleagues.

How we 'frame' mystery shopping in our minds and in the minds of the colleagues likely to be featured on film or audio file is crucial.

The following are examples of positive framing:

- It is the customer experience we are interested in, not the individual being filmed or recorded. We get a really good understanding of what happens for our customers from this type of programme.
- We might be able to improve some of our processes and improve customer service quality.
- Sharing best practice allows our colleagues to learn from each other.
- Noticeably good performances by colleagues can be rewarded.
- Opportunities for personal development may come from this in the form of training or additional support.

Inevitably, there are benefits and limitations to a coaching approach that relies on recorded mystery shopping materials.

Mystery shopping coaching

Benefits	Limitations
Improved likelihood of common perspectives of coach and coachee	Coaching session usually several weeks after the event
Observations verifiable	Requires planning
Can be replayed repeatedly	Relative cost of one-to-one coaching
Opportunities to share with colleagues and replicate excellence	

9

judgement or observation?

In order for you to effectively coach someone, there needs to be an agreed standard of behaviour that you are expecting. This will normally be provided by the customer service standards, or a specific set of work instructions or procedures your colleagues are expected to follow. In the case of visual or telephone mystery shopping, the reports reflect the expected standards of behaviour for the customer-facing team.

The goal of a Continue & Begin coach is to help the coachee strengthen his or her ego through the identification of positive *continue to* behaviours, and to tease out a small number of ambitions for *begin to* behavioural change, where the coachee believes it is helpful to do so. Behavioural change is most likely to be achieved when it is realistic and specific enough to be acted upon.

Coaching in your customer-facing organisation should be based upon observation – either the coachee's self awareness or the coach's personal observations, or, if you are fortunate enough, through the medium of video evidence or telephone recordings made as part of a professionally managed mystery shopping programme. It should not be about personal inference, 'mind reading' or making assumptions.

● **Observation** (or **fact**) is based on observed behaviour, which is either seen or heard.

● **Judgement** (or **mind reading**) invites argument and defensiveness and is not based on fact.

Example:

When the customer asked about other sizes you were not very helpful. You weren't interested in trying to make a sale.

This is **mind reading**, and therefore a **judgement.**

When the customer asked about other sizes you didn't make eye contact and you left the customer alone on the sales floor.

This is an **observation** of **fact.**

Listed below are a series of comments. Decide whether they are based on **judgement** (J) or **observation** (Ob).

1. *I was watching you for some time with that customer – you did not pay attention to her.*   J ☐   Ob ☐

2. *I saw you talking to that new member of staff about refunds and you weren't very friendly.*   J ☐   Ob ☐

3. *When you were using the computer, you stayed focused on the task. You didn't look up and make eye contact with the customer who was a metre away from you.*

   J ☐ Ob ☐

4. *You did a good job with that demonstration.*

   J ☐ Ob ☐

5. *When the customer asked you about tariffs, you smiled at him, put down your paperwork and walked with him to the display.* J ☐ Ob ☐

6. *"You didn't make eye contact with that customer when she asked you about the choice of fabric."* J ☐ Ob ☐

7. *"You handled that complaint really well."* J ☐ Ob ☐

8. *"When the customer asked you about finance you didn't maintain eye contact. There was an opportunity to up-sell and you answered with a single word."* J ☐ Ob ☐

9. *"You asked four questions to find out what the customer really needed and then left the customer for about five minutes while she decided on the colour. When you came back to check on the customer you asked if she had made a decision and then you suggested a link sale item."*

   J ☐ Ob ☐

Answers are provided in the Appendix to this book.

10

the structure of well-done-ness

In Question 4 of the 'Judgement or observation?' exercise above, the coach says, "You did a good job with that demonstration." Most people would agree that this is a judgement, even though it is a positive message. Of course, positive messages like this still have a beneficial effect on a coachee.

I refer to this type of positive, judgemental praise as 'Mars Bar Praise'. When you eat a Mars Bar your blood sugar level takes a massive leap and you are filled with energy. It's a sugar rush. An energy rush also happens with a strong caffeine drink. But it doesn't last long.

Mars Bar praise is common in most organisations. This occurs when managers give a quick 'well done' to a member of staff. We all like to be given praise for our work and it makes us feel good, at least for a little while – just like the 'energy rush' you get from chocolate or caffeine. The challenge is that often we don't really understand the specifics of our behaviour or actions that have resulted in the 'well done'.

If someone is to repeat an excellent piece of behaviour, it is important that he or she know precisely what it was that made it so good. This is what I call the Structure of Well-Done-Ness™.

I ask new coaches and managers to consider the Structure of Well-Done-Ness as the key to effective coaching. If a coachee can be helped to understand the precise activity that we wish to reinforce through praise, then he or she can embed that learning and repeat it again at a later date, knowing that that specific piece of behaviour has contributed to good performance – in this case excellence in customer service.

Consider education as an example. A few years ago I was working in my office at home when my (then) 18-year-old son Martin came home from surfing on our nearby beach. It was a school day and although I knew he had a light timetable as he approached his exams, I thought I should remind him of the importance of his studies. I decided to ask him how he was doing with his school coursework. As Martin stood by the surf shack where my kids kept their boards, I asked him, "How's school going, Mart?"

Martin was dripping with seawater, was peeling out of his wetsuit and clearly did not have educational matters at the forefront of his mind at the time. Clumsy and poor timing on my part!

"What?" he said.

By now I was in proper 'Father' mode and decided to see the conversation through.

N. I just wondered how you are getting on. It's not long till exam time, is it?

M. Couple of months. It's OK.

N. Had any grades back for coursework?

M. Yeah, I got an A for Physics.

N. Excellent! How did you get the A?

M. What do you mean?

N. I mean, what was it you did that meant it was worthy of an A grade?

M. Er... dunno. Just got an A!

N. Can I see the assignment?

M. It's on my desk.

I went to the study and found the assignment Mart was referring to. On the top of the front page there was an 'A' circled and a handwritten comment, "Well done!"

N. Mart, who's your physics teacher?

M. Woody.

N. Who?

M. Mr. Wood.

N. I've got a suggestion for you. When you see Mr. Wood, ask him to explain to you what, specifically, you did in that assignment that caused him to consider it an A grade. Mart, when you ask him, the word 'specifically' is very important, OK?

M. OK. I've got physics tomorrow, I'll ask him.

Sure enough, the next day I came home from my work to find Martin beaming.

M. I spoke to Woody, Dad.

N. Oh, yeah? What did he say?

M. He said that he gave me an A grade because I followed the analysis format he showed us for answering these types of assignment questions. He said that I'd used the formula he'd shown us and had got the calculation right. And he said that I'd structured my report in the way he'd asked us to, with terms of reference, an introduction, findings, conclusions, recommendations, appendices and a bibliography. He said if I did all that the next time with an assignment, I'd almost certainly get another A.

N. Nice. Now you know the Structure of Well-Done-Ness for your physics assignments. Well done!

M. Cheers, Dad. Epic.

This is such a simple notion, and yet few managers and team leaders use the Structure of Well-Done-Ness nearly enough to help and coach their people to consistently sustain excellence in their work. Rely on Mars Bar praise at your peril.

11
motivation vs movement

Fred Herzberg coined the phrase KITA in his work on motivational psychology in the 1960s. KITA, or Kick In The Arse, was Herzberg's definition of the kind of motivational encouragement given by some managers to their people. He distinguished between positive KITAs: rewards, bonus incentives, thank you's, etc.; and negative KITAs: including disciplinary actions, relationship changes, criticism, reduced financial rewards, and other punitive actions.

Herzberg argued that managers and leaders can get people to *temporarily* do 'virtually anything' if they make the KITA positive enough, or equally by contrast, painful enough. Herzberg knew that a shift in behaviour could be achieved by the application of a sufficiently strong KITA. Herzberg's point, though, was that this behavioural shift is nothing more than a Pavlovian reaction (Pavlov's dog) or a stimulus-response, like Skinner's operant conditioning.

Herzberg called this 'movement' and proposed that movement was a temporary response to the KITA. Herzberg suggested that if a manager wanted subsequent movement he would have to apply another KITA, and that over time the KITAs would need to become more intense as the employee becomes conditioned to the original level of incentive. KITAs are 'done' to people.

Motivation, by contrast, is a personal construct. It is as individual as the people employed within the business. The key to unlocking the full potential of an employee is to understand the Emotional Driver™ he or she has.

Emotional Drivers™ relate to a person's movement away from pain and towards pleasure motivators. Each employee is driven by an individualised set of motivational influences.

Motivation comes from within the individual. Motivation is a set of personal Emotional Drivers™ which are far more influential, certainly over the long term, than any KITA, whether positive or negative – unless of course the KITAs are perceived as life threatening to self or loved ones.

Herzberg's primary 'motivators' for his investigative subject group (200 accountants) still make sense:

- achievement
- recognition for achievement
- interest in the work itself
- responsibility
- advancement

Understanding the Emotional Drivers™ for people's urge to succeed at work does not require KITA activity. I suggest it is far more effective to use the coachee's model of motivation than to use an imposed 'movement' strategy.

The approach is simple enough: find out the Emotional Driver™ of the coachee by conversational questioning (without 'therapy') and use that understanding to help the coachee achieve the results she desires.

12

behaviour breeds behaviour

As coaches, managers or leaders, we are in positions of influence. The influence we have is as much by our behaviour as it is through our words. When we work with organisations, we can pretty quickly assess the likelihood of a new working methodology being implemented in a consistent fashion and sustained successfully just by the behaviours of senior people.

We come across some leaders and we just know it's not going to work out. Sometimes we will uncover pockets of leadership out in the field that are clearly not being performance managed. The behaviour of these managers impacts directly on their people and causes them to act in a similar way. It's similar to the influence that parents and older siblings have on youngsters: it is 'acquired behaviour'.

We are pretty good at spotting the negative people in an organisation or work team. We can generally identify them within a matter of seconds, and certainly within minutes, of meeting them.

In my coaching work with customer service and sales professionals, I encourage the executives and managers to adopt a positive approach to the opportunities for personal change and to build on strengths rather than examining weaknesses. We choose to use language that negates the negative. We talk about how people could be *even better* than they already are in areas where they feel they could improve even further.

We know how easy it is to slip back into negative 'whingeing'. Sadly, some leaders of men and women at work seem pre-programmed to whine about the circumstances they find themselves in. We also know how unproductive and damaging that way of thinking can be. Some of our team leader and manager delegates struggle with maintaining a positive frame of mind over a few hours, never mind a career!

Now, obviously nobody reading this book (!) has any of the following behavioural tendencies, but let's explore them and discover if you know anyone in your organisation who may, from time to time, behave in these energy-sapping ways.

● PLOMs (Poor Little Old Me)
PLOMs are the kind of people who sigh a lot and have a despondent outlook on life. They usually have a hunched or slumped physiology that has the useful effect of allowing only a minimal amount of oxygen into the lungs, thereby limiting the blood flow of nutrients and energy. This is a great way to feel downbeat and hard-done-by.

- ### R-BUTs (Ah-Buts)
  R-BUTs are excellent if you want to test your thinking for any flaws, partial thinking or implementation 'risk assessment', because these people will find fault with most new initiatives. "Ah, but, what you obviously haven't thought of is..." These folk are not known for their creative or solution-oriented thinking.

- ### CAVE People (Continually Against Virtually Everything)
  CAVE people are easy to identify. They will be the ones who disagree with the new project. *Which* new project? It doesn't matter because they will be arguing against it. Usually good mates with the R-BUTs.

- ### ICBAs (Ick-Bahs)
  ICBAs are unlikely to be enthusiastic about new plans, because as an ICBA would say, "I Can't Be Arsed."

- ### Mood Hoovers, Deirdre Dysons and Private Frasers
  These people come from the same family of psychic vampires: they all suck the energy and goodness from any workplace. If you're really old (like me) you'll remember that Private Fraser was the old Scottish funeral director in Dad's Army who would eagerly suggest at each moment of difficulty, "We're all doomed!"

  Be careful using this one, especially the Deirdre Dyson version. We were in mid-flow describing this characteristic of depression-inducing managers to a group of delegates when we realised that the project sponsor, a senior player in the business, was called... you've got it: Deirdre!

- ● MGs (Moaners and Groaners) and BMWs (Bastards, Moaners and Whingers)
  Speaks for itself really. We've all worked with them at some time or another.

- ● 20/20s (Twenty/Twentys)
  20/20s are a common breed. These are the managers and leaders within an organisation who have the great benefit of experience. This is wonderful, except that on the odd occasion you will meet a manager who hasn't got 20 years' experience at all: he or she has one year's experience repeated 20 times over, the same every year. These folk are not known for their flexibility of thought or behaviour. One manager in a rather staid public sector organisation with low staff turnover and a high stability rate explained to us that her organisation had quite a few 20/20s, but even more 40/40s!

What We Want Are EGGs!

For EGG people *Everything is Going to go Great!*

EGG managers are the kind of people we all want to have as leaders and managers. These people make excellent coaches because they focus on the positives of what could be, rather than the likelihood of 'problems' and failure.

Hope is a powerful motivator for people, including coaches.

It was Eric Hoffer who wrote about the influence of hope on a group of people:

> *Fear of the future causes us to lean against and cling to the present, while faith in the future renders us receptive to change.* The True Believer, Harper & Row, 1951, p. 9.

Being EGG-ish is a great way to encourage, to enthuse, to inspire and to motivate people towards positive action. We all know the truism that we tend to get what we focus on. EGG coaches focus on positive outcomes, on solutions and success.

Go on, EGG it!

13

accentuating
the positive

People are most receptive to behavioural change when they are relaxed and feel good about themselves. It is in these psychologically fertile conditions that employees feel strong and secure enough to consider alternative personal behaviours as opportunities to become *even better*. Ego strengthening is therefore at the heart of the Continue & Begin model of coaching.

By starting from the (explicitly expressed) premise that the coachee is already doing really well in certain areas, we can create a mindset within him or her that enables him or her to feel good, before we get anywhere near a change plan.

It is important to record these areas of performance excellence and to emphasise how valuable these competences are for the coachee and for the organisation in which he or she operates.

We propose two coaching models that address a number of common scenarios. The coaching models are:

1. Continue & Begin
2. Kipling Coaching™

The main focus of this book is on the well-proven and highly effective Continue & Begin approach. Kipling Coaching is included for the sake of completeness, and for use in a very specific circumstance.

Common opportunities to coach customer-facing colleagues in a sales and service environment include scenarios such as:

1. The customer service performance of the coachee, as recently observed by the coach.

2. The customer service performance of the coachee, as featured on a visual mystery shopping film.

3. The customer service performance of the coachee, as featured on a telephone audio file.

4. The ambitions the coachee has for enhancing a specific skill.

14

continue & begin™
coaching model

In scenarios 1, 2 and 3 above, I recommend the Continue & Begin coaching model. If the coach has recently observed the coachee in action, has viewed his or her performance on video, or has listened to him or her on audio file, this model works really well.

I developed the Continue & Begin coaching model in 2002 when I first began working with visual mystery shopping material. It was pretty obvious from the start that visual footage is a wonderful resource for helping people to recognise what they are good at, and the areas where they can become 'even better'.

I am proud to report that since it was developed in 2002, Continue & Begin has been introduced and implemented within an increasing number of class-leading organisations, including world-class automotive manufacturers, leading financial institutions, retail household names, public authorities and small to medium-sized businesses across the UK.

Continue & Begin recognises that the coachee is already exhibiting excellence in a number of areas of customer service and celebrates this by formally recording those behaviours that the coachee wishes to *continue to* deliver on a consistent basis. We encourage coaches to identify as many *continue to* behaviours as possible – certainly five or six and possibly more.

Sometimes it takes a while for the coachee to identify what he or she is good at! The British national culture tends to inhibit our willingness to tell others about what we believe we excel at. Some people even struggle to tell *themselves* what they are good at!

A good Continue & Begin coach will tease out these repressed competences and will create what hypnotherapists call a 'yes set', where the coachee feels increasingly confident in expressing himself or herself about areas in which he or she excels. The 'yes set' is a great way to develop a momentum of thinking about a given subject. For more on 'yes sets', read the work on hypnotic phenomena by Dr. Milton Erickson (the acknowledged father of modern hypnotherapy), or Dimitri Udnadze's research on the Theory of Set.

Once we have the coachee feeling good about himself or herself, we can ask him or her to confirm that he or she wishes to *continue to* deliver excellence in the behaviours and skills that have been identified. This is the Simpsons question that usually leads to a *Doh!* response: of course the coachee wishes to continue to do well! It is important here that the coachee actually records these *continue to* behaviours on an action plan sheet that we provide. This has the effect of embedding the behaviours in the mind of the coachee.

Writing down commitments (which is effectively what we are doing here) is a powerful, and well-proven, methodology that has been employed in goal setting and goal mapping for many years. For more on goal mapping, read Brian Mayne's excellent work at www.liftinternational.com.

continue & begin™ personal strategies

Coachee	
Coach	
Date	
Personal Strategies	Continue to:
	Begin to:
	Commitment is doing the thing you said you would do, long after the mood you said it in has left you!

Writing down goals seems, somehow, to result in their achievement. Sometimes we get too analytical in trying to understand the theoretical logic that proves that something works. If it works, it works. Take our advice on this one – it works, so just enjoy it and benefit from it. If you really must know more about goal-directed thinking and behaviour, then read Alfred Adler and what he called the *teleological* nature of man.

Once we have a set of *continue to* behaviours recorded, the coachee is now in a psychological position where he or she is feeling strong enough to consider the areas of operation in which he or she *could be even better*.

Notice the positive construct of the language pattern *could be even better*. There is no suggestion that the coachee is in any way deficient or inadequate. On the contrary, the language pattern hints at the coachee already being competent and that he or she has an opportunity to improve that competence to an even higher level. This is the power of this model! At no stage is the coachee confronted with criticism from the coach.

The strategy for identifying areas in which the coachee could *begin to* do even better is simply to ask the coachee what he or she thinks. In the case of visual or telephone mystery shopping, this is a simple task, as the coachee invariably blurts out his or her inadequacies right at the start of the meeting, after the video or audio file has been played back.

For some reason, people who have seen themselves on film (and to a lesser extent have heard themselves on audio file) immediately go into self-flagellation mode. They will publicly beat themselves up over the apparently 'dreadful' performance they have just seen or heard themselves deliver.

Let's explore how this works in practice. After the video has been viewed, or the audio file listened to, a typical discussion will go something like this:

Coach. Well, what do you think?

Coachee. It was awful; I can't believe I didn't smile. I looked so miserable. The customer must have thought I was so rude, and I looked so scruffy, my hair was awful. And I didn't up-sell when I could have done. It was terrible!

Coach. I'm sure there are a few things you might want to do differently next time. Let's park those (over here) for a moment. What were you really pleased about?

Coachee. What do you mean?

Coach. What did you see or hear that made you think, "Yes, I did that well, I'm pleased with that"?

Coachee. Nothing.

Coach. Nothing? Nothing at all?

Coachee. Not really.

Coach. There must be something you thought you did well.

Coachee. I suppose I acknowledged the customer quite quickly.

Coach. Yes you did – I noticed that, very prompt. What else did you do well?

Coachee. I was wearing my name badge!

Coach. That's right you were. What else?

Coachee. I asked him a couple of questions about what he wanted. I found out what he *didn't* want too, because he told me. And I offered him a bag. I sometimes forget that.

Coach. They were excellent questions. And yes, you did offer him a bag. What else?

Coachee. That's about it I think. Oh, I got all his details so I can send him the newsletter when it comes out.

Coach. Well done! Excellent! Yes, you did do that. Let's just summarise what you did well: there was... well, can you remember?

Coachee. I think so. There was the acknowledgement, I asked some good questions, I offered him a bag and I got his details – oh, and I was wearing my name badge!

Coach. Well done. Pretty impressive when you think it through, isn't it?

Coachee. Yes, I suppose so.

Coach. I guess you would like to continue to do those things well, wouldn't you?

Coachee. Well, yes, of course.

Coach. OK, let's write them down then on this action plan. The things you want to continue to do well, every time you meet a customer. Here's a pen.

Coachee. OK.

Coach. Now, there were a couple of things that you said you wanted to do differently next time. Remind me, what were they? I think we parked them over here...

Coachee. Oh, those... they were...

And only then do we begin the process of discussing the things the coachee would like to *begin to* do differently. We find that as a general rule it is best to find a 2:1 ratio, where we help the coachee to identify twice as many *continue to* behaviours as *begin to* behaviours. If we can get to a ratio of 6:3 that is about perfect, with six *continue to* and three *begin to* behaviours.

The temptation for the coach and the coachee is to deal with all the many and varied *begin to* behaviours immediately! This is an ineffective strategy. Let us explain why.

It was the psychologist George Miller who identified the 'seven plus or minus two' model of conscious thinking. Miller established that most people can handle (at a conscious level of thought) between five and nine ideas at any one time. Some people in some situations can cope with up to nine ideas or concepts, whilst for others in some environments five is quite enough. If we ask a featured coachee to change the way he or she operates in a dozen different or new ways of operating, he or she will be overawed, confused, and almost certainly unable to deliver the goods.

It's much better to identify just a small number of *begin to* behaviours, never more than three, and to take action on these three so that they become areas of competence really quickly. We will often ask,

Have you ever eaten elephant steak?

To which the answer is normally "No."

We will suggest:

You need a VERY BIG PLATE!' That's why it's important to eat the elephant in small helpings that can be easily digested, one at a time.

Once we have a set of *continue to* and *begin to* behaviours in place, written down by the coachee, we can move on to the final part of the coaching session itself, before the coachee goes back to work to make it happen. We get just the tiniest bit direct and look deep into the eyes of the coachee and say:

Are you serious about these 'continue and begins' or are you just messing about?

The response is usually a definite, "Yes! Of course I'm serious about them!" and we can then be confident that the coachee will actually take action rather than talk about taking action.

What we know about *begin to* behaviours is that when the coaching has been managed effectively and change begins to occur, those *begin to* behaviours have a habit of becoming *continue to* behaviours pretty quickly!

15

kipling coaching

For scenario 4 above,

The ambitions the coachee has for enhancing a specific skill,

I would recommend a slightly different approach, using what I call Kipling Coaching. Put simply, this is a coaching model that works best when the coachee has already identified a specific behaviour or goal that he or she wishes to achieve and needs a bit of help in getting there. He or she has a specific *ambition*.

The model makes use of four of Rudyard Kipling's six honest serving men, which he made famous in the *Just So Stories* (1902).

> *I keep six honest serving-men*
> *(They taught me all I knew);*
> *Their names are What and Why and When*
> *And How and Where and Who.*

Once we have identified what it is the coachee wants to achieve, we can use four of Kipling's honest serving men: Why? How?

What? and When? Each question is made more probing by the addition of specificity.

Identification of ambition

What is it you want to achieve? This is the specific behaviour or ability the coachee has mapped out as an 'ambition'.

1. **Achievement of higher logical level of understanding**
   Why?
   Why *specifically?*
   Why do you want to do this?
   What is the benefit to you?

2. **Achievement of strategy**
   How?
   How *specifically?*
   How will you achieve your ambition?
   What strategies will you employ?
   How will they help you in achieving your ambition?

3. **Mop up strategies**
   What else?
   What else *specifically?*
   What else will you need to do?
   Beyond those things you have identified already, what else is required to make this happen?

4. **Timescale strategy**
   When?
   When *specifically?*
   When will you take action?
   When are the key milestones on your time line?
   When will you review progress?
   When will you know you have succeeded?

Remember, the Kipling model is best used for scenarios where the coachee has already decided precisely what he or she wants to achieve, in very specific terms, and is interested in help in achieving her ambition. It takes a little longer than Continue & Begin and is not designed for rapid coaching on the sales floor. It has its place as a personal development framework, and is great at clarifying the thinking of the coachee.

The model is simple to use and easy to remember, because it has just four key steps to recall. The importance of the word 'specifically' is that it acts as a fuzzy- thinking buster. Fuzzy think- ing is commonplace in most people's plans for change and bene- fits from a nudge in the direction of the specific. If we can guide the coachee to think in a more productive and specific fashion, we are helping him or her to be much more targeted in his or her actions, which, in turn, will create more beneficial outcomes.

16
language that hinders

Words have the power to build up or to tear down. There are a few common pitfalls of 'danger language' that can damage coaching effectiveness. Chief amongst these are the following:

1. Shoulds and musts

Should, must, ought to, have to, have got to, and need to, are words or phases that demand something of an individual. Readers familiar with Rational Emotive Behaviour Therapy (REBT) will recognise the nature of these words and their common association with what Albert Ellis called irrational beliefs.

By using such demanding language the coach is (perhaps without even knowing) placing an irrational suggestion into the mind of the coachee.

In reality, the coachee doesn't *have to* do anything at all. There may be repercussions for him or her if he or she doesn't do what is being demanded, but the fact remains that the coachee can do whatever he or she damn well chooses! The leverage gained by using such emotive language is akin to Herzberg's KITAs and has no place in an organisation that cares for its people. It's not even particularly effective. We know that compliance with KITAs is an untrue allegiance. It merely creates temporary compliance. As one of our colleagues sometimes comments,

*That manager just **shoulds** all over his staff. It's very messy.*

In REBT, people who consistently use this type of language (typically about themselves, incidentally) are known as *must debators*, or *mustabators*, depending on how risqué you want to be. *Mustabator* language has no place in coaching.

2. Why can't you?

This is one of our favourites. When we sit alongside a new coach, or a relatively experienced coach who has been poorly trained, we hear this language pattern time and time again. "Why can't you do it?" or "Why do you think you are having difficulties with this?" This is the worst possible question a coach can ask a coachee.

When a coachee is asked, "Why can't you X?" the individual goes on a search through his or her mind to find the equivalent of a computer folder that has the heading, "Why I Can't X." Once found, it is simply a case of opening the folder up and finding all the files that have good reasons for "Why I Can't X." It's hugely effective at confirming that you can't do something.

When we ask someone, "Why can't you?", there is a presupposition implicit in the question, that is: "We both know you can't do it." This is not the stuff of possibility or personal choice! As George Zalucki says (Mind and Emotions audio tape) in our slight paraphrase,

The Thinker thinks and the Prover proves. If the Thinker thinks I can't the Prover has to prove you are right.

Asking someone why he or she can't do something just reinforces why he or she can't, even when with a little resourceful thinking and some behavioural changes, he or she probably can. Use "Why can't you?" and you will perform poorly as a coach.

3. The But Monster™

The But Monster™ is a word that joins two sentences together. In coaching it can also act as a destructive rapport breaker.

Imagine a scenario – Pam, a customer services manager, meets with a customer services assistant, Tom, perhaps at an appraisal meeting, and proceeds to explain how *some* of his work has been *quite good* and that he has achieved *some* of his objectives. Maybe the manager goes on to add that other parts of Tom's work have been *quite good, too*. Now, imagine also that Pam (the manager) is using a spoken syntax that has a downward inflection to the end of each sentence – 'sentence dropping' as it is sometimes called.

The impact of the customer services manager's message is already disempowering for Tom. He has, remarkably, broken the code of the message, even before it is has been delivered completely – the employee knows instinctively that the next word to be uttered by the manager will be *'But...'* followed by a message that is either critical or negative, or both. How does he know this? By what means does he have the mind-reading capabilities to second-guess the manager's thinking?

The reality, of course, is that the customer services assistant has learned from his life experience that certain language patterns, combined with specific tonal, non-verbal, and pre-verbal messages, have a high statistical probability of leading to a specific form of communication after the *'But...'*.

Look closely at the following examples:

*You were quite friendly with the customer **but** you should have spent much more time on the phone with her.*

*Yes, when he called you did acknowledge him, **but** you ought to have used his name.*

*Your performance at the till was OK **but** you need to up-sell more while you are wrapping.*

Have you noticed the impact of the word **'but'** on what is being said? In the examples shown, the use of the word negates all that goes before it.

The word **'but'** is an example of conjunctive grammar; that is, a word that links sentences together. *So, yet, as, because, until* and *after* are other examples. In training seminars we have fun with our delegates, teasing individuals with our tonality and use of the But Monster, as we call it.

To illustrate this during our training seminars, we will often select an individual and start by saying something like,

Chris, so far today you have contributed quite well (downward inflection)...

And you have made some useful points (downward inflection)...

And you have helped your colleagues (downward inflection)...

Pause... and smile...

Within seconds the poor victim will say "**But...**"

In coaching, we recognise that the But Monster erases all the good positive language that precedes it. As one young manager told us,

"You just know that everything before the But Monster is bullshit."

Psychologically, we know that all the previous stuff about contributing well and making helpful contributions is just waffle which is there to offset the pain of the message that is about to follow the But Monster.

We know from stress studies that modern work-related stress has the same effect on our bodies being chased by a sabre-toothed tiger had on our ancestors – we prepare to fight, flight or 'play dead'. Our autonomous nervous system kicks in at the first sign of threat and causes us to react physically in readiness for a survival strategy. This was an effective auto-response system for our species in prehistoric times.

There aren't too many sabre-toothed tigers around these days (excepting some particularly aggressive managers I know) and yet we still prepare ourselves for emotional strain by tensing muscles, increasing blood flow through heightened blood pressure, and releasing sweat to prepare our body-cooling systems. The But Monster is just one of many dangerous creatures lurking in the lexicon of our business language.

Watch out, too for the But Monster in disguise. Any threatened species adapts to its environment and the But Monster is no different. It will sometimes disguise itself as *however* or *although* – cunning, eh! These are diluted forms of the But Monster that can still cause serious damage to rapport. Beware the But Monster and its relatives! Fortunately, use of the But Monster can be controlled so that it is used properly to negate things that perhaps *should be* negated, e.g.,

*OK, so you failed the exam, **but** you can always take it again next week.*

In coaching, use of the But Monster will cause pain. The coachee will tense up his or her muscles, unconsciously, in readiness for the optional responses of fight, flight or play dead. This causes physical discomfort as well as psychological distress. People who are tense do not readily absorb new ideas. Being open and curious requires a state of relaxation and the But Monster creates the opposite effect in a coachee.

4. Healthy Alternatives to the But Monster™

When you decide to avoid using the word **'but'** you can either 'break the sentence' and start a new one, or you can substitute the word *and* or *even though* in its place. Either works really well. Using the phrase 'even better' is a nice way to stay positive, and of course an upward tonality breathes positivity into any dialogue. It's important to keep the tone up.

Let's try those sentences again:

*You were quite friendly with the customer **and** what would be great next time is if you could spend even more time on the phone with her.*

*Yes, when he called you did acknowledge him, **and** next time you could use his name to build rapport even more quickly.*

Your performance at the till was OK! (Full stop, deep breath, new sentence.) *You know, you could make your performance even better by up-selling while you are wrapping.*

The But Monster bites! Please avoid using it when coaching.

5. Miscellaneous hinderers

Some language patterns are too obvious to describe in detail, and yet we hear them consistently being used. Here are a few that make us cringe (or smile depending on our mood!):

How many times have I told you this?
(Try helping me in a different way then!)

I don't mean to criticise...
(But I'm about to...)

You could have done much better...
(Thanks for the encouragement!)

With the greatest of respect...
(I have none for you.)

If I were you...
(Well you're not, so shut up.)

17

language
that helps

We know that some language patterns can be especially empowering for a coachee. When we give individuals the freedom to think for themselves, in a guided format, we allow them to create their own possibilities, rather than relying on being spoon-fed behavioural change requirements that have the effect of being a KITA in disguise. It's far better for the employee to determine his or her own strategy for change.

Some of the following constructive questions and conversational prompts have the effect of opening up possibilities for a coachee. They work really well when combined with an observed performance or with video and telephone mystery shopping:

Opening lines

Well, what do you think?

How do you think that went?

What did you really like?

What were you really pleased with?

Observations to prompt discussion

When you were... I noticed that...

One of the things you did was...

One of the things you said was...

You asked lots of questions to find out ...

I think I heard you say...

What I really liked was...

Encourage and challenge

I wonder, is there anything you could have done to help make that even better?

Right, if you had to do it again....

I'm curious, if you were that customer....

Yes, I agree.... What specifically could you have done?

18

can't to can™

We all have limiting beliefs about some things. When those limiting beliefs get in the way of us doing our jobs well, it's time to take some belief-busting action!

The Can't to Can™ model is a really cool tool for helping people get out of a thinking rut and move towards more productive thinking and behaviour. The model has a sequence that takes an individual from where he or she is now – stuck in negativity – towards a place of opportunity and possibility, with four simple questions.

We all use self-talk, chatting away to ourselves virtually constantly. Sometimes our self-talk leads us to negativity or disempowering thinking. What seems to happen is that we get stuck in what we call No-Through-Road Thinking™, where we think we can go no further in terms of options or choices.

We've all been there and it can seem a desperate place.

I (NDK) wasn't happy with this as a psychological phenomenon so I decided to change it for myself and for anyone else who wanted to benefit. What I did was to take a couple of excellent questions from therapy, now common in NLP, (I call them freedom questions) and blend them in with a sequence of other questions that together make a powerful change tool for coaches, managers, sports players, teenagers, employees, therapists and just about anybody who wants to get out of the No-Through-Road Thinking dilemma.

What you will see below is a word flow version of the Can't to Can™ model that I developed as a mechanism to help people change. A visual version is presented later. The power of the model is immense and, I believe, should be taught in schools to children and to trainee teachers at universities around the world.

This is how it works:

1. **Identify the 'I can't'**
   Identify the coachee's No-Through-Road Thinking, e.g., "I can't up-sell warranties."

2. **Avoid 'why'**
   Avoid the temptation to ask, "Why can't you up-sell warranties?" You now know what happens when you ask the 'Why?' question.

3. **First freedom question**
   Ask the first 'freedom question' to raise the topic of possibility: "What would happen if you could do that thing you say you can't?" It is quite normal to have to ask this question a few times, as the initial programmed response from the coachee is to repeat his original message, "Yes, but I told you, I can't!"

4. Identify benefit

Once you've broken through "I can't" and encouraged the coachee to at least consider the first freedom question, the response will usually identify a specific benefit that being able to do that thing would create. In this case it might be something like, "I'll be able to earn more commission – and keep my manager off my back, too."

5. Ask the Simpsons

Once you get the positive response, ask the Simpsons' *Doh!* question: "Well, would you like that?" If the coachee has any urge to change his or her work life for the better the answer will be, "Yes, of course I would!"

6. Second freedom question

We then ask the second freedom question, "Well, what would have to happen to make that happen?" The only possible answer (apart from "I don't know") to this question is a positive suggestion of some sort, typically a fairly high-level generality such as, "I'd need to feel more confident about it." This is a common response from many who are having difficulty achieving work performance targets or achieving competence in a given skill or procedure.

What happens now is the really cool part.

We have helped the coachee reach a stage where he or she has begun to consider options other than not being able to do that thing that he or she says he or she can't do, and we have accessed a response that is positive in a generic sense. Now we are about to probe a little deeper and clear away the generalisations that the coachee has presented. All we do is repeat the same question again! This is the common flow of responses:

Coach. *"What would have to happen for you to feel more confident in up-selling warranties?"*

Coachee. *"I'd need to know a bit more about the way the insurance policies work. I wasn't there the day it was explained."* The coachee will often feel the need to justify why he or she can't do that thing, and that's cool. We don't need to know why he or she can't; we just want to help him or her to do it in future, right?

Coach. *"Oh, OK! So, what would have to happen for you to know more about the insurances?"*

Coachee. *"I'd need some training."*

Coach. *"Yes, that's right, I guess you would."* The 'that's right' language pattern is drawn from Ericksonian hypnosis, when he confirms that the patient is making useful choices, thereby deepening rapport and encouraging the patient to continue to participate in this fruitful adventure!

"What would have to happen for you to get some training then?"

Note how the same core question (What would have to happen?) is being asked again and again. Elegant coaches will change the question very slightly so that it is not perceived as being repeated.

Coachee. *"I suppose I should ask my manager. She could arrange it for me."*

Coach. *"Oh, OK, cool. How could you go about asking her?"*

Coachee. *"I'll just ask her when I see her."*

7. Time target

We now have an agreed action plan mapped out. What we don't have is any form of timescale or sense of urgency.

Coach. *"Excellent, that's a good idea. When will that be?"*

Coachee. *"Oh, pretty soon, I should think."* (This is a time ordinal generalisation – there is no specificity about when.)

Coach. *"How soon, specifically?"* ('Specifically' is a most useful precision tool in coaching.)

Coach. *"Tomorrow."*

Coach. *"Come on! What time tomorrow, specifically?"*

Coachee. *"Oh, OK! Nine o'clock, as soon as I get in!"*

8. Summarise

Now we need to summarise our agreement and reinforce the plan.

Coach. *"Well done! So. Let me just check what you've told me...* ("What you've told me" is an important piece of leverage in gaining commitment)... *you said that if you could sell more warranties it would help you earn more commission and keep your manager off your back too, is that correct?"*

Coachee. *"That's right."* What we are in the process of doing now is building up a 'yes set' of responses that will lead us to the final killer question to gain commitment. This statement by the coachee is 'yes set' statement number 1.

Coach. *"And you said that you would like that, is that right?"*

Coachee. *"Doh! Yeees!"* ('yes set' 2)

Coach. *"OK, and you said that if you speak to your manager tomorrow morning at 9 o'clock ...*(Nine o'clock was the language the coachee used, so that's the language we will use too, rather than, for example, 9 a.m.)... *then you could arrange some training, and that that training would give you the product knowledge, to give you the confidence, to be able to sell lots of lovely warranties and earn stacks of commission – you won't need to worry about keeping your boss off your back when you do that! Have I got that all right?"*

Coachee. *"Yes you have."* ('yes set' 3)

Coach. *"Brilliant! So all I need to know from you (name) is this...* (this is the one part of the process where we go out of rapport towards a more authoritarian approach, with deep eye contact and 'serious' face)... *are you serious about making this change or are you just messing about?"*

Coachee. *"I'm serious!"* ('yes set' 4)

9. Killer question

Here comes the killer question to buy-in commitment...

Coach. *"Good, because I will do everything I can to help you make this happen, if you are truly committed. Are you?"* (Killer question)

Coachee. *"I am."*

Coach. *"Good. Go and make it happen."*

The flow chart opposite describes this visually. Read it from the bottom up!

Can't to can™ model

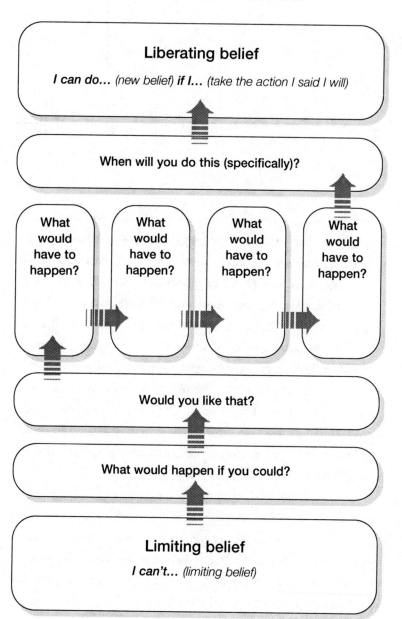

19

sitting with nellie

Knowing what to do is different to doing what you know.

Where visual or telephone mystery shopping is being used as a resource for the coaching process, really smart customer service businesses make sure that an experienced coach (a *'Supercoach'*) sits alongside the first-time coach on his or her very first coaching session. This helps to ensure new skills are applied in an effective, and damage-free, manner. Clients regularly report the benefit of this 'safety net'. We refer to this as Sitting with Nellie.

An effective strategy for Sitting with Nellie is for the new coach and his or her more experienced colleague – the *Supercoach* – to meet up prior to the coaching session to decide on how best to run the pre-arranged coaching session with the colleague who has been featured on film.

The *Supercoach* will ask the new coach how he or she plans to manage the coaching session and will 'coach' the new coach on how the session can offer optimum value for both the coachee and the organisation. Through discussion, the two will agree on a revised strategy (or maybe confirm that the original plan was fine) and then will conduct the session with the coachee.

The new coach will introduce the *Supercoach* as someone who is there to monitor the way that he or she conducts the coaching session and is in no way interested in the performance of the coachee as featured on film. It is the *process* employed by the new coach that the *Supercoach* is interested in.

After the session, the *Supercoach* coaches the new coach (!) on how he or she conducted the session and how he or she might repeat successes or change to more effective strategies when next conducting a coaching session.

Key to this process is that the coaching methodology employed by the *Supercoach* should be the same as the agreed Continue to & Begin coaching model (or, if appropriate, Kipling Coaching). This has the effect of reinforcing the learning for the new coach. We have lots of fun acting as *Supercoach* in this format as we wait for the new coach to recognise the methodology being employed. When the penny drops, the new coach will exclaim, "Hang on a minute, I know what you're doing!" and burst into laughter. The impact in embedding the learning is fabulous.

We encourage the new coach to develop his or her own learning plan, in the organisation's house style, and then to use it as a means of gradually (or even rapidly!) improving his or her coaching skills.

20
team coaching

One-to-one coaching is great for creating behaviour shifts in one person; that is, the person being coached. What it doesn't do is cover off a wider audience of colleagues. Team coaching, or 'one-to-many' as it is sometimes called, provides an opportunity to spread the benefits across a work group.

How can you gain a massive return on investment from just one coaching session?

In observed behaviour coaching, one-to-many activities can be challenging to undertake, because colleagues may not have seen or heard the originating performance of the coachee.

One-to-many coaching is far more user-friendly when visual, telephone or email mystery shopping is employed by an organisation. In such circumstances, the coaching process uses the mystery shop recording as the reference point for discussion. There is no need to remember what happened with the customer because it can be watched, heard, or read, over and over again. This makes for an excellent reference point for colleagues of the featured coachee and provides a valuable personal development resource.

When one-to-many coaching is conducted well, using mystery shopping recordings, the return on investment for the organisation is immense.

The most effective approach is to use the video footage, audio recording or email copy as the focus for a team of colleagues. It is essential to make sure the featured coachee agrees to share the recording of him or her in action, as well as the action plan, with his or her teammates. This agreement is crucial if the coaching philosophy of mutual trust is to be maintained.

The key here is the extent to which the one-to-one coaching session is perceived by the coachee as having been productive and nurturing. The more beneficial the one-to-one coaching session to the coachee, the more likely he or she is to agree to share the material with colleagues.

The first time a coaching session is run using mystery shopping programme material is usually the most uncertain time for the coach, almost as much as for the featured coachee. This is why the Sitting with Nellie option makes such good sense. The new coach is inevitably unsure of some aspects of the new coaching skills he or she has learnt and this uncertainty will be apparent to the coachee – if not directly, than at the unconscious level of communication.

There is a selling job to be done by the coach at the end of the one-to-one coaching session. Once the action plan is complete and the coachee has made a commitment to the Continue & Begin behaviours, it is time for the coach to ask two killer questions:

Are you willing to share the contents of your action plan with your work-team colleagues?

Are you willing to let your work-team colleagues watch the video/listen to the telephone call/read the email correspondence?

If the answer to these questions is "Yes", then a one-to-many session can be set up for a time convenient for the workgroup and the business.

The best team coaching sessions usually involve a degree of fun, or at least a relaxed environment and a few nice treats. Some organisations go for beer and pizza after work once a quarter when their mystery shopping materials arrive. Other companies like to avoid alcohol and enjoy cappuccino coffees and cakes. Others are more a bacon sandwich kind of culture.

Some organisations run their team coaching sessions before work, some afterwards. Some wait until the full team is in attendance, while others run mini one-to-many sessions, with two or three colleagues participating in the process.

Whatever approach is adopted, the rule of thumb that seems to create a success pattern is to allow the featured employee to explain the contents of the film, audio file or email before it is revealed to his or her workmates. The coachee explains what he or she has learnt from the experience of watching, listening to, or reading his or her customer service performance at a given moment in time.

When the coachee explains what he or she has experienced during the coaching process and how this has helped to determine a plan that ensures he or she will continue to do the things he or she has done well, and identifies opportunities for his or her customer service performance to be *even better*, his or her colleagues will recognise that there are real benefits from the new coaching approach.

There is almost always a deep empathy for the featured member of staff from colleagues, as each of the gathered employees engage in internal dialogue along the lines of, "It could have been me, and it might be me next time."

Narrow and deep, shallow and wide

One-to-many coaching sessions usually result in the coachee's work-team colleagues identifying a number of customer service or sales behaviours that they consider to be their personal strengths. They will also identify maybe one or two areas of performance where they recognise their own fallibility and have an opportunity to improve on their service quality.

One-to-one coaching creates enormous behavioural shifts in the featured coachee, with 'narrow and deep' change in one person. One-to-many coaching sessions tend to create 'shallow and wide' behaviour changes, with a small number of personal Continue & Begin activities identified by the wider work group.

The impact of a well-run team coaching event can be phenomenal.

Helpful hints for one-to-many coaching sessions

- Think about how best you can promote your team coaching event in a positive and fun way. Make it a night to remember (for all the right reasons).

- Consider the best environment for your group coaching sessions – are there enough places for everyone to sit? Is it informal or formal?

- What sort of culture do you have? Is it pizza and beer, coffee and buns or tea and bacon sandwiches?

- Ensure anyone who is likely to cause any conflict is sitting near to you (or whoever is running the session). Troublemakers find it difficult to be troublesome when they are close to the meeting leader. Avoid sitting directly opposite the troublemakers – this only serves to accentuate the confrontation. Similarly, if you have any quieter types, try getting them in front of you and they will be more inclined to contribute.

- You can control who speaks by asking specific questions to specific people.

- If any louder people are overpowering the quieter types, thank them for their contributions and ask, "What do other people think?" or say with a smile, "(Name) – you know, you have some excellent ideas! They are really helpful and I need to find out what other people think too." Turn to the rest of the group and ask specific people for contributions.

- Use the same coaching question sets for the group as you did in the one-to-one coaching session – as each answer is given, encourage the rest of the group to comment further by saying, "Good – anything else?"

● Encourage the group to think about what they do. Have them suggest alternative ways of doing the same thing – what are the tips and tricks they use? "How do you do that?" "What's the best way of doing that?"

● When completing action plans, concentrate on the elements of their own performance that the session has made them think about. Encourage them to identify what they do particularly well and wish to *continue to* do and list a small number of behaviours. Then identify one or two behaviours they feel they would like to *begin to* do differently.

● Ask the group to share some of their *continue to* and *begin to* examples.

● Go through the Commitment Mantra that says, "Commitment is doing the thing you said you would do, long after the mood you said it in has left you!"

PART B

continue & begin™ workshop transcript

CONTINUE & BEGIN™
WORKSHOP TRANSCRIPT

When you exhibit excellence in a specific behavioural skill,
what is the structure of your Well-Done-Ness?

Nick Drake-Knight

What follows is a transcribed narrative extracted from a one-day training seminar facilitated by Nick Drake-Knight, and recorded live. The seminar helped a group of managers from a diverse range of commercial and retail businesses to develop their coaching skills using a number of coaching methodologies, including Drake-Knight's unique Continue & Begin™ coaching model. As part of the seminar, delegates also learnt how to use covertly recorded visual and telephone mystery shopping video and audio files as coaching resources.

The training seminar emphasised that the coaching skills being presented could be used equally effectively in day-to-day behavioural situations, where a manager has observed a colleague in action. It's not necessary to have mystery shopping video footage or telephone audio file recordings to effectively coach someone using the Continue & Begin model.

The transcript, recorded live at a coaching seminar, works at a number of levels:

- as a learning experience for managers of retail staff, automotive sales executives and financial services advisers – and many other commercial managers
- as a knowledge transfer event for professional trainers
- as an illustration to business leaders on how a day-to-day coaching culture in organisations can revolutionise business performance
- as an introduction to the phenomenal power of video or telephone mystery shopping as a service improvement tool

The transcript is packed full of stories, illustrations, indirect suggestions and embedded commands. Some of these are apparent in written form, while many are embedded within the tonality and analogue marking that Nick uses to make messages 'stick' within the minds of delegates. The event introduces language patterns drawn from Neuro-Linguistic Programming (NLP) and other therapeutic disciplines to create changes in working behaviour.

By using linguistic patterns that influence and create sustainability, Nick develops the capabilities of managers and team leaders to go on and coach their team members using innovative and high-impact methods developed over many years of trial, error and lots of laughter. Nick mixes teasing and mild provocation with jokes, gentle regression, intriguing hints at something deeper, and messages of such profound significance that many delegates have referred to his training as the best management development they have ever experienced.

The transcript presents some of the key instructional sessions from the day.

21

introduction

NDK. Good morning. Welcome to *Continue & Begin*™ Let's have a chat about the big picture, shall we?

Today *will* be a stretch for you folks. I will be asking you to consider what lies beyond your comfort zones. You will have the opportunity to explore new territory and to venture into experiences that may seem unusual or strange.

At all times you will be nurtured and encouraged. I will make it my personal mission to ensure you are safe physically, psychologically and emotionally. At the end of the seminar you will be able to coach your colleagues *even better* than you already do. And we'll have some fun too, because you wouldn't want to enjoy yourself at work, would you?

(Delegates' nervous laughter.)

I know that some of you are very experienced coaches, some of you are less experienced, and some of you are in between the two. The expectation on our part is that there is a degree of skill set already present here in the room today. So we start from the premise that you are already good, or very good, or fantastic!

For those of you who are fantastic, we are going to give you some content, and train you in how to use that content effectively. For those of you who are starting from a different place, we will give you the opportunity to brush up on some of your existing coaching skills. There are lots of opportunities during the day for you to pick my brains, and those of my colleagues. So please feel free at any point where you may feel a little uncomfortable to come forward and ask. We recognise that there is a spectrum of experience, abilities and styles within the room and we also recognise that you are starting at different places. Happy with that? Good.

It's my job to take you through the *Continue & Begin*™ programme. Your task when you leave here tomorrow will be to go out and coach your store, dealership and branch colleagues in their retail outlets.

Let's just be clear on this. I understand that some of you will be running your first coaching events next week, is that correct?

Sean. I won't actually be running *Continue & Begin*™ but I am explaining it to our regional managers in the South on Tuesday. If they go for it, I'll be coaching dealership sales executives later this month.

NDK. OK. Anyone else?

Sarah. That's me next Wednesday. I'll be coaching some of our people in Glasgow, so I'm rather keen to learn how to do it!

NDK. OK, we're talking about delivering something that is not far away folks; we're talking about running coaching sessions that for some of you are only a few days away. So, we will need you today to be *in the room*, as well as in the room – you understand what I mean by that? Sometimes we're in the room and we're not *in the room*. We need you to be in the room and *in the room*.

In a moment we'll run through the day in outline. This afternoon you'll experience the doing bit. We have a saying here, "Knowing what to do is **not** the same as doing what you know." You have to experience things in order to truly understand them, and to embed new skills. Otherwise people say, "Yeah, I read that book."

This afternoon you get to do what you know – or at least what you will know by lunchtime. The *Continue & Begin*™ programme is participative and active in the morning, but it is in the afternoon that you will do the thing you are learning to do, and that is coach!

By the close of play of this *Continue & Begin*™ event you'll be able to go away and coach people using this awesome stuff *(picks up video mystery shopping DVD)*. Or, simply by watching and listening to your colleagues operate, in their customer-facing roles, you'll be able to apply the coaching skills and knowledge we will teach you today.

Now, who's been in a training and development role for a number of years? OK, you'll know the difference between coaching and training.

Training is a structured inductive process. It's led by a trainer and is designed to transfer knowledge or skills to help people perform specific job tasks.

Coaching is different. Coaching is an ongoing process that helps people become better at a skill they have already been trained in, and at which they wish to become *even better*. Coaching is about helping people who already have ability and knowledge and would benefit from further improving their performance. Primarily it is a process used to change behaviour.

With the skills you will learn today, you'll be able to coach people based on what you see and hear them do. There's something else though: we'll introduce you to the phenomenal power of visual and telephone mystery shopping. This thing here *(DVD of mystery shop video footage)*, used carefully, can do amazing things for people. Amazing things. And here's the health warning... you can do great *good* with this mystery shopping material. You can change the way people operate at work for the better. You can change their lives: the way they perceive themselves, their outlook on life. You can do all those things with this. It's a wonderfully empowering tool. Or... you can cause great damage. I've seen people on both ends of that scale, and when people get hurt by this it causes deep, deep scars. So, as a starting point for today, when you're running your first coaching sessions – next Wednesday for you, Sarah – please remember just how sensitive this stuff is. Happy with that as a starting point? OK, let's rock!

Let's think about what this training programme is all about, shall we? By the end of this *Continue & Begin*™ event you will go away capable of coaching people really effectively using this fabulous mystery shopping film or telephone recording. But there's more than that.

If you go away knowing how to use mystery shopping films or telephone recordings once a quarter – because that's the typical frequency of a mystery shop programme – frankly, it's not a great return on investment, is it? Four times a year to use the new skills that you've been given? It's not a great return considering how much your time costs, the time cost of the people being coached, and especially considering how much I'm charging you for my time today! If I were the big boss I'd think, "That's pretty expensive." Ah, but that's not all we're going to achieve today.

What you're going to be able to do is coach whether you've got a DVD, a telephone recording, a copy of an email, or whether you just see your colleagues on the sales floor doing their stuff. These are new coaching skills you can use every day!

The key, ladies and gentlemen, is to create a culture in your organisations where it is the norm to engage in coaching each other; where people feel OK about discussing how well they are operating as a customer service or sales professional, and how they can become *even better*. It's about people reflecting on the customer service they have just facilitated and considering what went well, and what could be done differently next time. It's about accepting that sometimes we get things wrong – we are all fallible human beings – and that we can strive for continuous and never-ending improvement in the quality of service we offer to customers and potential customers.

So *Continue & Begin*™ is not just about mystery shopping, it's not just about waiting for videos or telephone recordings to arrive, it's about discovering people doing things right every single day. What we want you to be able to do is to go away and use the coaching skills you're going to learn from me today and use them every single day with your people. I don't want you getting hung up on, "This is all about mystery shopping" – yes, of course it is and what a fantastic resource – *and* we're going to be able to use it as an everyday coaching technique as well.

You don't have to wait for a DVD to appear, OK? Does this make sense?

(Nods from delegates.)

NDK. Good.

22

the model
of excellence

NDK. Ladies and gentlemen, there are three component parts to world-class performance in what we might call the *customer service experience.*

The first one is this... world leaders in any business, in terms of service excellence, have explicit standards in place for service processes or sales processes. That is to say, they make it clear to their people precisely what is expected of them in their day-to-day jobs interacting with customers. Precisely. Now some organisations are excellent in making clear the explicit expectations of their people. Other organisations are *less excellent.*

On their own, though, explicit standards are not enough. They're very important, because clearly people need to know what's expected of them, and managers need to be able to monitor that performance, but they're not enough.

The second thing is this: you know when I go and work with organisations, the very first thing the operations director will say to me is this, he or she will say,

Across our national estate there are (typically about three hundred stores or branches) *some pockets of excellence. I've got parts of my national or regional business which are absolutely first rate, I can't fault them. I've also got huge acres, fields, of mediocrity, of average-ness, where it's 'OK'. And I've also got just a few pits of despair. It's just dreadful. What I want across my national estate is consistency. I want everyone to perform to those high levels.*

That's the request that I hear time and time again, and world-class operators have that consistency right across their estate.

But it's not enough. You see, you can achieve consistency through training. You can get a degree of commonality of performance, at least to begin with, by training people in a certain way. But here's the challenge, folks. Because at the end of the training session what often happens when it's been a really fun, buzzy, inspirational training event? How are people feeling in terms of motivation at the end of that day?

Siobhan. Wonderful..

John. Full of motivation.

Nuj. They're up for it.

NDK. That's right, and you've been on those programmes haven't you?

(Nods from delegates.)

NDK. You're going to change the world, aren't you! And then you get back to work, and what happens?

Jack. A couple of days and it's back to normal.

NDK. Exactly. All the dross and the detail and the day-to-day stuff that we have to deal with... it all conspires against our best intentions, doesn't it?

(Nods from delegates.)

It doesn't take long before it's forgotten, does it? Now, here's the challenge, and this is what happens in a lot of organisations. They get some service standards, they get some fabulous ones; they then roll out the training sessions – fantastic! *(pause)* But it's like mud against the wall, because within a few days most of it begins to slide off.

It's a complete waste of time. I call it parachute training. You know, organisations employ people like me at huge expense, we get parachuted in, we do all sorts of fab training, we're heli-coptered out again, and then what? The learning goes. It's a complete waste of time. Hey! The money is nice for the training companies, but when you're measured on the impact of training on performance over the long term, it's not good enough. So what we've got to have, and what these world-class operators have, is *sustainability.* And that means keeping consistency going long after the mood at the end of the course has died away. How do you do that? I'll explain.

You achieve sustainability, ladies and gentlemen, through having a coaching capability locally based, in your stores, or branches, or dealerships, or whatever business model you oper-ate with. A coaching capability that results in your local leaders saying to service staff,

Hey Tracy, how are getting on with meet and greet, with qualification, with product demonstration? I was watching you just now and I noticed a couple of things you did really well. Do you fancy a cup of tea? We can go through that together so you can recognise what you did so well. I think there might something we can do to make it even better, too. Fancy a five-minute chat?

When you can create a locally supportive coaching skill set and culture, *then* you'll achieve sustainability. Is this making sense?

(Nods from delegates.)

Good, because that is when service standards will be delivered consistently, day in, day out, across the organisation. Then you're on a winner. And that's why those top players are top players.

23
positivity

Let's get into coaching itself. This is where we start. After today, everything you're going to do with your people will start from a platform of positivity. This whole event is built around the premise that your people are already good at what they do.

OK, just have a look at that flippy over there… incidentally, the walls are pretty bare at the moment but they'll be full by the end of the day, you'd better believe it… and incidentally, whenever someone says 'incidentally', it's rarely an incidental point they're making. Think about that one.

People learn best when they're relaxed and having a good time. They learn best when they're confident and they're feeling good about themselves. And – something called solution-focused thinking, or goal-oriented thinking – they learn best when they've got a plan of action in their minds. It's really, really important that people are feeling confident. So, we start from a platform of positivity. I've already done it with you this morning – listen to the language patterns today. Listen to the words and the sequence of the words I use.

I said to you this morning that you were already really good, didn't I? I said some of you were fantastic, some of you were good, and some of you were just starting out. The premise is that you're already good at what you do. So you're going to do this with the people you're going to coach in your stores, your branches and your dealerships. You're going to tell them that you know that they're already doing a grand job. What the session with them is about is to help them – watch the movement *(raises left arm outwards to the left at 45 degrees towards ceiling)* – to become 'even better than they already are'. Listen to the language pattern: 'even better than they already are'. Are you with me on this?

(Nods from delegates.)

NDK. Good.

We start with ego strengthening. The whole programme – the coaching philosophy – is built on the premise that if we can get people's egos strong they're more likely to take on board improvement strategies. When people are beating themselves up and are low in confidence they have low self-worth, low self-image, low self-esteem. And you kick them. What's it going to do to them? It's going to make them feel even lower, isn't it?

So, what we do is, we make them feel fantastic and when they're feeling great we ask them, "Would you like to feel even greater?" and they say, "Oh, yes please!" And we say, "OK, let's find out how we can do that." And that's what we're going to learn to do today, so that at the sessions you'll be running, you can help people identify what they can do to become *even better* than they already are.

24

what do you want to learn?

NDK. Let's start out with Martin. Martin? What do you want out of today? Why are you here?

Martin. I heard about this course from some colleagues and I wanted to experience it. I want to understand the concepts behind your coaching model and how we can use it to create great coaches in our dealerships.

Siobhan. I want to be able to deliver a really good session and help my colleagues become *even better* at being professional sales people.

NDK. Nice language pattern, Siobhan!

Nuj. Two things for me. I want to understand the content, and I also want to enhance my coaching delivery skills.

Chris. I heard about your course from a friend who'd been on it. He said it was the best training event he'd ever been on, so I thought I'd better come along and have a look for myself. I want to be trained by you, Nick!

NDK. OK, no pressure then. Thanks Chris. Just sit back, close your eyes and relax. I'll wake you up when you've been trained.

(Laughter.)

Sarah. I'm an area manager for *(employer name)*. I want to understand your coaching model, but I also want to radically improve the coaching skills of the managers in the region I manage.

Tony. I want to improve my coaching ability.

Jack. I'm an area manager too. I want to get an idea of how I can help my branch managers to go out there and perform really, really well. More specifically, I want to be able to use key phrases to coach effectively with the mystery shopping films.

NDK. Ah, key phrases. Listen folks, for the benefit of you guys, OK – semantics is the meaning of words, syntax is the structure of sentences. You said something there that's very important. Do you know what it was?

Jack. Er, no…

NDK. You said the word 'specifically'.

Jack. Did I?

NDK. Yes, and a very useful word that is, too. That word is going to mean more and more and more to you as we progress through today. The word 'specifically'. We use a lot of what we call 'fuzzy' language. You know English is an incredibly blunt instrument. Anybody here go skiing? Any skiers? Yes? How many different types of snow are there? Daisy?

Daisy. Er, powder, compact, icy, slushy…

Nuj. You get yellow snow!

(Laughter.)

NDK. Never eat yellow snow! You get many different types of snow. And how many words do we have in English for snow? One. We have lots of adjectives we can add to the noun 'snow' to describe the different types – including yellow snow, Nuj – but we have only one word for the noun. How many words do the Inuit nations have?

John. 50?

NDK. Many. The Hottentots used to have a great counting system centuries ago – they counted one, two… many! It's a great numerical system. I think it would simplify our lives if we used *that* arithmetic model. Imagine, "What is the sales target for March, Tony?" "Well Nick, I think the target for March is 'many'." "Blimey Tony, we'd better get selling then…"

(Laughter.)

NDK. English is an incredibly blunt instrument: incredibly blunt. And what you discover during the coaching process is that our communication accuracy is pretty poor. And so I'm going to encourage you to use this word more and more... "What do you mean by that... sssspppecifically?" Think about that – the structure of language. And the meaning of words... we're going to explore this more and more. OK, who else?

Jenny. I want to get the language used across our business, not just in coaching sessions. I've heard about the positive language you use on this course and I want our whole organisation to be communicating in this way. At a personal level I want to attempt to improve my coaching.

25

do or no do, no 'try'

NDK. Listen to the language folks... Jenny, you're going to... what was the word you used... can you remember? 'Attempt.' We're going to talk about language, the power of language, and examples of the tentative language that we 'sometimes' 'try' to use.

Today folks, we are going to do those things that you want to do. It's going to happen. We're not going to 'try'; we're going to do it. It's going to happen. We're not going to 'hopefully' do it. When you're helping your people to change the way they operate, they're going to do it, they're not going to 'try' to do it, because that's tentative. It won't happen.

Let me explain why it's so important to do, not 'try'. Your unconscious mind is like a lazy teenager. It will lie on the couch all day if it can, eating pizza and watching TV. It's programmed to do a few important things like protect you from danger – that's why you can smell smoke and fire so easily – and it's programmed to run your autonomic nervous system; you know, your breathing, your pulse, the oxygenation of your blood vessels, that sort of thing. It's very good at those autopilot activities. Otherwise though, it's bone idle and will do the least possible work unless you tell it to with real intent.

It responds well to firm instructions. It will do what you want, but you must give it clear, unambiguous, direct instructions. This is why... hey, have any of you ever had to get up really, really early in the morning for an important event and you've set the alarm super early, and you've set your phone alarm too, and you've found another alarm just in case... and then what happens?

Chris. You wake up just before the alarm goes off.

NDK. That's right. And why is that? It's because just for once in your life you gave your unconscious mind such a strong instruction that it sat up straight on the couch, put down the pizza and said, "OK, will do!" and then it did what you'd programmed it to do. Listen folks, George Zalucki said, what do you think would happen if the Sergeant Major said to his troops, "Would you like to do some marching today, boys?"

(Laughter.)

NDK. Do you think they would march? Of course not! The instruction has to be firm and direct. And this is why when we 'try' to do something we usually fail. Like Yoda said in Star Wars, "There is no try – do or no do." Or something like that.

Hopefully, maybe, possibly, I hope so, it should do, I might, I'll give it a go – these are all tentative language phrases that send meek and mild messages to the teenager on the couch in your mind. Guess what the teenager says? "Yeah, yeah," and does nothing. Listen, I know, I've got hundreds of teenagers. At least it feels like hundreds. They're lovely young people and very expensive.

Start making tentative language a thing of the past for you ladies and gentlemen. Do or no do.

26
kita movement

NDK. OK, let's find out about the psychologist Fred Herzberg's thinking about coaching. He didn't realise he was talking about coaching, but it's what Gregory Bateson called a 'pattern which connects'; that is, it applies equally well to a completely different set of circumstances. Bateson was a genius!

Fred Herzberg was interested in motivational psychology within an industrial setting. We are interested in coaching our people to achieve *even higher* levels of performance than they currently achieve.

Anyway, Fred Herzberg. What Fred said was this: he said, "Look, I can get you, Nuj, to do *virtually* anything. Not anything, but *virtually* anything, if the incentive is big enough. And I can get you, Jackie, to do *virtually* anything if I make the fear of pain, or pain itself, big enough." He called this a KITA. *(Writes on flipchart.)*

Any ideas? No?

A Kick In The Arse! He said, I can get you to do virtually anything if I make the KITA positive enough or negative enough. Incidentally – remember what I said about 'incidentally'? – the fear of pain is a fear of future pain. You can't be fearful of now, you can only be fearful of what might happen soon, or in the future. This is an important distinction and a learning point for coaches from the field of therapy. People are fearful or frightened of what *might* happen as the next step after 'now'.

And what he said was this... here's the challenge... if I want you to do it again, what have I got to do? What have I got to do, Nuj?

Nuj. Kick again?

NDK. That's right, I've got to give you another kick. Except, probably, I've got to make the KITA even harder this time. In your case, Nuj, it was a positive KITA, wasn't it? I would have to make the positive KITA even more attractive to you. Even more alluring... than last time. Because we kind of get a bit used to getting the same old positive KITAs, don't we? So the reward has to be even bigger. Or, in the case of a negative KITA... the fear of future pain... has to become even more scary! And this is what happens... he said, you get 'movement'. I can get you to move. I can get you to move, Daisy. And if I want you to move again, I've got to give you another KITA, either a positive one or a negative one. And you'll move. So, the thing is, in a coaching context, by using KITAs we can create movement. *(Long pause.)* But it's not motivation. Because, motivation comes from where?

Crystal. From within.

NDK. That's right, Crystal, it comes from inside. From within people. And that's why it's impossible to 'motivate people'. You cannot *motivate* people. You can't do it! It has to come from inside. We can create climate and atmospheric conditions that make it easier for people to feel motivated, but you can't press a button. "Where's the motivation button on you, Sarah? I'm just going to come and press it." There isn't one. It comes from inside people.

What we've got is a fantastic tool to help people find that internal motivation. It's this thing here *(holds up DVD)*. Because when you see yourself on this, something quite remarkable happens. Frankly, you don't need a coach, you don't need an area manager, you don't need a trainer... you don't need anybody to tell you that there's an opportunity to do things differently, because you already know. Because what happens when people see this thing, and they turn the film off we ask a simple question, "Well, what did you think?" There's no downward tone, there's no upward tone... it's a flat tone. We give nothing away in our tone that comments on the calibre of the performance we've both just watched on film. "Well, what did you think?" And this is what will happen, 99 times out of a 100... the person featured on film... listen to the language... the person *featured* on film... did I say captured or caught? No. The person *featured* on film will go into self-flagellation-beat-myself-up mode when we ask the question... let's have the mantra folks..."Well, what did you think?" and they'll say, "Oooh! I don't believe I did that, oh, no, look at my hair, and I need to lose 17 stone, oh, no!"

(Laughter.)

They'll go into beat-up mode. Now, what was it I said about ego, self-esteem, all that sort of stuff? What could we do, what are the choices, if we were cruel, heartless souls?

John. Kick 'em.

NDK. Yes, we could give them a few KITAs, couldn't we? Let's do that – yeah! Or, we could say something much more healthy, which is, "Look, I'm sure there are a few things you might want to do differently. Let's just park those for a moment." *(Makes movement to place imaginary 'box' to one side).* "What were you really pleased with?"

So what I want you to understand is the power of this *(holds up DVD)* to help people to become motivated themselves from within.

27
draw a townhouse

NDK. OK, we're going to draw a townhouse now. We get to do all sorts of exciting things today. You can go home and you can tell your kids that you've been at work doing drawings. I need four volunteers… we'll have Sarah, we'll have Jenny, we'll have Nuj, and we'll have Colin. Well volunteered. So folks, I need you to find a partner who's going to help you, in a sort of consultant mode, for this tricky task that lies ahead of you.

Found someone? If you haven't, just choose someone you don't know, and go up to them and say, "I like the look of you, please be my advisory consultant on this drawing exercise." Done it? Good. Here we go… you'll need some flipchart paper and what you're going to do in one-and-a-half minutes is to draw a townhouse; you know, one of those houses you get in the middle of a town, maybe in a mews area or something like that. Anyway, you only have one-and-a-half minutes, so get ready… everybody got flippy paper and a marker pen? OK… go!

(Delegates complete drawings of townhouse in allotted time.)

NDK. OK, what you're going to see now is a demonstration of four very distinctly different coaching styles. Pay attention please and concentrate. I'll exhibit each of the four styles once each. Let's start with Sarah.

(Approaches Sarah and sits down next to her. Coaching illustration 1.)

NDK. Hi Sarah, how's it going? A bit of a trek wasn't it for you today, all that way down from Glasgow? How did you get down here?

Sarah. I came by car.

NDK. Oh, OK. What route did you take, because I never know which way to come down.

Sarah. Just straight down the motorway really, then onto the M6.

NDK. OK. So, how long did that take you?

Sarah. About four hours altogether, I suppose. I took it steady.

NDK. Quite a drive. I used to work in Glasgow. Whereabouts do you live?

Sarah. Well, it's not really Glasgow. It's really Greenock, but not many people know where that is, so I say Glasgow. It's easier.

NDK. I know Greenock. I had a chum of mine, years ago, he used to live in Gourock. That's not far from Greenock.

Sarah. Just a few miles, aye. Do you know the area then?

NDK. Well it was along time ago. I went biking there last year. I went up to Oban and over to Barra. I went through Gourock.

Sarah. What did you think of Barra?

NDK. Well, actually I thought it was very nice, but the ferry took forever! I met a guy in a café on South Uist and he asked where I came from. I said the Isle of Wight and he asked how I'd got to South Uist. I told him, on my Kawasaki. I said how the ferry had taken five-and-a-half hours and he said in this beautiful sing-song accent, "Oh, that will be the new ferry then." He said the old one used to take 13 hours! It was lovely there. Anyway, nice drawing. Thanks Sarah, catch you later.

(Gets up and moves. Sits next to Jenny. Coaching illustration 2.)

NDK. Ok, Jenny, so what were you looking to do here? What was your plan?

Jenny. Well, just to draw a house that I think reflects my understanding of a townhouse. I'm not entirely happy with it.

NDK. OK, so this represents your thoughts on what you think a townhouse should look like?

Jenny. Yes. I didn't have quite enough time to complete it to the standards I would have liked, but this is pretty much what I had in mind.

NDK. Right. So, take me though the key features of your drawing.

Jenny. Well, I've tried to create an image that is slightly 3D in effect. I've drawn it from the perspective of an angle to make it more lifelike.

NDK. I can see that. What else?

Jenny. Well, here is the door, and these are the three windows.

NDK. Why did you decide to go for three windows?

Jenny. Pretty predictable, I suppose! I think that's all you're likely to get on the front of a townhouse, but as you can see I've put a skylight in the roof.

NDK. Yes, I can see that, too. And what are these?

Jenny. They are window boxes with flowers in.

NDK. I see. OK. What are you really pleased with about this drawing?

Jenny. Not much really.

NDK. There must be something?

Jenny. Well, I suppose the window boxes are a good idea.

NDK. Yes, a very good idea. What else are you pleased with?

Jenny. Erm, well, the skylight in the roof is pretty cool.

NDK. Very cool! What else is good?

Jenny. The smoke coming out of the chimney makes it feel homey.

NDK. A nice touch. OK, so, in summary, you're pleased with the window boxes?

Jenny. Yes.

NDK. The skylight?

Jenny. Yes.

NDK. And you're pleased with the smoke coming out of the chimney?

Jenny. Yes.

NDK. What else?

Jenny. I thought the curtains were quite stylish.

NDK. The curtains are very stylish! So, let me just check. If you were to draw the townhouse again, you'd keep all those details you've just mentioned, would you?

Jenny. Yes, I think I would.

NDK. Excellent. OK, you said you weren't entirely happy with the drawing. I only gave you a minute and a half, which was hardly fair, was it?

Jenny. Not really. Not to do a really good job.

NDK. OK. If I had given you more time, what would you have done differently?

Jenny. I think I wouldn't have gone for the 3D effect. I think it looks childlike. It would be better if it were drawn in a plan style. That would look more professional.

NDK. Anything else?

Jenny. Yes. More colour next time.

NDK. Fine. OK. Let me just check what you've told me, and see if I've got this right. If you were asked to draw a townhouse again, and I were to give you a little more time, you would do some of the things you did the first time again, is that right?

Jenny. Yes, the window boxes, the smoke, the skylight and the curtains.

NDK. Great. And you'd probably do a couple of things differently? What were they?

Jenny. I'd do it in plan format and add in some colours.

NDK. Excellent. So, if I gave you five minutes now, you could do an *even better* job?

Jenny. Definitely.

NDK. You have a plan to continue to do the four things you liked, and to begin to do two things differently. Is that correct?

Jenny. That's right, yes.

NDK. Are you serious about doing this even better next time, or are you just messing about?

Jenny. No, I'm serious.

NDK. You can do the drawing again this afternoon at two o'clock, OK? And remember to include the four things you'll continue to do well, and the two things you'll begin to do differently. Up for it?

Jenny. OK, definitely. Is that a coaching action plan by any chance?

NDK. It's exactly that Jenny, exactly that. Nice work.

Jenny. Thank you, Nick.

(Gets up and moves. Sits next to Nuj. Coaching illustration 3.)

NDK. All right, Nuj – what's this then?

Nuj. It's my drawing of a townhouse.

(Lifts up flipchart with drawing, turns it to show rest of group and smirks.)

NDK. Call that a townhouse?

Nuj. Yes. I think it's quite smart.

NDK. Smart? Are you serious? Have you always had a problem with drawing?

(Drops flipchart to table with dismissive air and shakes head. Laughter from delegates.)

NDK. Let me explain to you what you should have done. What you should have done is laid it out more professionally. What you need to do, Nuj, is to put more effort into your work. You ought to have used more colours. When you do this sort of work you must be accurate, and you haven't been. If I were you I'd think long and hard about this. How many times did I tell you – this was supposed to be a townhouse and it's not, is it?

(Walks back to centre stage.)

NDK. So, there we are – four explicit coaching styles that we can discuss. What did you think?

Colin. That was only three. You forgot me.

NDK. Sorry?

Colin. You didn't coach me. You ignored me.

NDK. Did I? Oh, I'm so sorry, Colin. Yes, I did. I completely forgot all about you. Still, you got the idea, didn't you?

Colin. *(Smiling.)* Yes, I've got the idea!

NDK. OK. *(Shakes hands with Colin.)* Thanks for being a good sport Colin. What did it feel like being left out of the coaching?

Colin. Pretty horrible, actually. I realised quite soon that it was a set-up when you ignored me, but even then I felt awful. Like I wasn't getting the attention I wanted.

NDK. Even though Colin realised it was a set-up, he *still* felt bad. How about that folks? I've got to tell you, I've been doing this activity for years and sometimes the people who've been ignored still want their coaching session before the end of the seminar! Let it go, Colin, just let it go!

(Laughter.)

NDK. OK, what about the other coaching styles? Let's start chronologically. What was going on there with Sarah?

Martin. It was non-specific. It wasn't really about the subject. There was no real coaching. You were just being nice to her.

Dawn. You were building rapport, but you didn't address the issue you were there to deal with.

NDK. Deal with?

Dawn. You know, coach her on.

NDK. But Sarah is lovely! We had a very nice chat and we got on so well! We had a delightful time together, didn't we Sarah?

Sarah. Yes we did. It was about me and I liked that. But we didn't really address the task.

Nuj. I don't think you'll see any change in behaviour.

Martin. I thought you were avoiding the issue.

NDK. And that's what happens so often, folks. Coaching is about addressing the issues, not just building rapport. Of course, rapport is a vital part of the communication process, but an effective coaching session includes an element of challenge: a discussion about how the coachee can step beyond the current level of performance and become even more effective than he or she already is. Did you hear the tone? *Even more* effective. And you simply won't do that unless you address the issues.

OK. What about Jenny? What happened for you Jenny?

Jenny. You coached me. You asked me about what I thought. You got a commitment from me.

NDK. OK, listen to the language. The word that was used there by Jenny was 'commitment'. Remember that word, we'll be using it a lot today. In your packs, at the back, you'll see the commitment mantra, can you see it? "Commitment is doing the thing you said you would do, long after the mood you said it in has left you." That's a George Zalucki phrase. He's well worth a listen. You can check out his audio tapes on the inter-web-net-thing.

Siobhan. You gave her a really detailed coaching session. You asked her what she liked and what she didn't like.

Nuj. And you identified what she had done well, and what she wanted to do better next time.

NDK. Better?

Jenny. Actually, you said 'differently', not 'better'.

NDK. That's right, well spotted Jenny. You listened to the words. Remember what we said about ego strengthening? We want people to feel good about themselves. We want them to understand that they have *choice* in their actions and behaviours.

If we ask them how it could be better, there is what's called a 'presupposition' that it's currently not good. Most people who are stuck in a particular way of behaving believe they have no choice, or at best very little choice. In fact, if you think about it, two choices isn't a choice at all, it's a dilemma!

(Laughter.)

NDK. So, we encourage people to recognise that they have choice, and asking them how they could do it differently amplifies that message.

So then what happened?

Martin. You summarised the things she had identified as being well done, and those that she decided she wanted to be better at – sorry, 'do differently'.

NDK. Exactly. And I offered her my support in helping her achieve her ambitions. She needs to know that I'm backing her when it comes round to doing it again. What happened there, in fact, is that we experienced the very first example of what we call the Continue & Begin coaching model.

Jenny had four *continue to's*; that is, four behaviours she wants to continue to do well in similar circumstances, and two *begin to's*, that is, two behaviours that she has committed to begin to do differently from now on. And I'm there to help her if she needs me. Got it? Simple isn't it? And quick! That's the beauty of Continue & Begin: it takes only a few minutes and it's profoundly powerful. We'll come back to Continue & Begin on plenty more occasions today.

What about poor Nuj?

Sarah. You ridiculed him.

Siobhan. And you did it in front of others, too.

NDK. I know. I'm so sorry Nuj. *(Shakes hands.)* Will you accept my apology?

Nuj. No. I'm deeply hurt.

(Laughter.)

NDK. Quite rightly, too. Fortunately, none of you have ever experienced that style of coaching have you? *(Pause.)* Well, let's hope never again, eh?

Chris. Let's hope not.

NDK. What did you notice about the language I used?

Daisy. There were lots of 'need to' and 'shoulds' in there.

Jack. You were using aggressive language, in a bullying way.

NDK. Wow! Listen to the words I used with Nuj. 'Need to', 'should', 'have to', 'got to', 'ought to', 'must'…these are emotive words aren't they? Later on, we'll investigate the nature of language patterns and how they impact positively or negatively on the coaching process. OK. Useful?

Tony. Very.

NDK. Let's move on.

28

judgement
or observation

NDK. OK, let's just be clear on something here. In order for you to effectively coach someone, there needs to be an agreed standard of behaviour that you're expecting. Think about it. If employees don't understand what is expected of them, how do you expect them to achieve it? This is basic logic.

You see, I think it's a fundamental human right to have your job role and performance expectations explained to you!

Anyway, in the case of mystery shopping coaching, the mystery shopping measurement report will illustrate the standards of behaviour expected of the employee, in terms of customer service behaviours and the sales processes required by your businesses. If only it were always so explicit!

Your goal as a new coach is to provide guidance to your coaches on goal expectations that is informal and achievable, and specific enough to be acted upon. Now then, there are two examples here: one called a 'judgement' and one called an 'observation'. Observation is based on a fact, either seen or heard. With judgement we get argument. It's opinion. It's mind reading.

You know, Nuj, you just weren't interested in that last activity, were you? I could tell. "Oh, really?" you might say. "So for how long have you had the Mr. Spock mind-lock transference skills, Nick? Actually I *was* interested." No, you weren't. "Yes I was." No, you weren't. "Yes I was."

You see, as soon as we get into mind reading, we hit difficulties. It's a recipe for argument, confrontation and a really ineffective coaching session. Far better to stick to the facts. Use observation to highlight a behaviour that the coachee exhibited and use that as the reference point for your discussion.

Of course, we're really lucky with visual or telephone mystery shopping materials because we can refer to the film or audio file. If the coachee says, "I didn't do that, did I?" we can check by simply referring to the mystery shop. There's no need to argue over whether he or she did or didn't. It's there for us to refer back to. Pretty smart, eh?

As a general rule of thumb, if based on your comment you can get into an argument, it's almost certainly a judgement – an opinion. Let's have a look at these examples here.

(Runs through 'judgement or observation' activity – see Chapter 9.)

29

the structure of well-done-ness

NDK. Now, let's have a look at this specific example. "You did a really good job with that customer." Is that a judgement or observation?

Jack. A judgement.

NDK. Why?

Jack. Because we could argue over whether it was a good job or not.

NDK. Well done. Yes, we could argue over it, but surely it's a nice judgement, isn't it?

Siobhan. It's still a judgement.

NDK. Correct. It's what we call 'Mars Bar praise'. Let me explain. What happens to your blood sugar level when you eat a Mars Bar?

Crystal. It goes up.

NDK. It does. For how long, Crystal?

Crystal. Not long. A few minutes.

NDK. That's right. We get a short boost and then the energy levels begin to tail off pretty quickly. That's why it's important to keep eating lots of chocolate, at all times – isn't that right, girls?

(Laughter.)

NDK. Well, Mars Bar praise is just like that. Can I just check something? John, I reckon you must be well into your twenties, is that correct? Maybe 22 or 23?

(Laughter – John is well into his fifties.)

NDK. When the boss says, "Well done," it still feels good doesn't it?

John. Yes, of course.

NDK. And yet you're a grown up – what, maybe almost 30 or something?

(Laughter.)

NDK. And yet the praise still feels good. But the challenge is, Mars Bar praise doesn't last – and let's face it Sarah, if you're going to have some pleasure, you'd like it to last a decent amount of time, wouldn't you?

(Laughter. Sarah colours up with embarrassment.)

NDK. Mars Bar praise doesn't last because it's non-specific and not structured. It's just a sugar rush.

Let me tell you a story. I have lots of children. Hundreds of them. At least it feels like hundreds, especially when all their friends come round. They're all big and mostly grown up now. They're lovely young people and they're also very, very expensive. A few years ago I was working from home and my number two son – you have to number them when you've got as many as I have – he came home from surfing down at the beach. He was in the middle of A levels and had taken a break between his studies. I was in dutiful father mode and I said to him, "Hey Martin, how's school going?" He stood in the doorway with his wetsuit dripping onto the floor and his surfboard under his arm. "What?" he said.

Dad. "How's your coursework going?"

Martin. "OK."

D. "Had any grades back recently?"

M. "Yeah."

D. "Which ones?"

M. "Physics. I got an A."

D. "Wow! Can I have a look?"

Sure enough, there was Mart's physics assignment with a stamped 'A' circled on the front page and the handwritten message, "Well done!"

D. "Nice! How did you get that?"

M. "What do you mean?"

D. "What did you do to get an A?"

M. "Dunno. Just did."

D. "Yes, but what specifically was it about your piece of work that got you the A grade?"

M. "Dunno really."

D. "Who's your Physics teacher?"

M. "Woody."

D. "Who?"

M. "Mr. Woods."

D. "How about you ask him what it was that caused him to think your work was worth an A grade?"

M. "OK, I will."

The next day Martin caught up with me…

M. "I spoke to Woody, Dad."

D. "Oh yes?"

M. "He said I got an A because I used the methodology he showed us, I used the equation he taught us, I explained my calculation and presented the report in the format he suggested. He said if I did the next piece of coursework in the same way I'd probably get another A grade, too."

D. "Great! That's the Structure of Well-Done-Ness, Martin!"

At work, if you want to develop your people effectively, and sustain their performance at a really high level, Mars Bar praise is not enough. When people do things well at work and you praise them, they need to know what, specifically, they did that made the piece of work so impressive. They need to know their Structure of Well-Done-Ness. Make sense?

(Nods from delegates.)

Folks, you are going to be at a place, by lunchtime, where you are going to *know what to do* to make your first coaching session really productive for your coachee. But that is not the same as *doing what you know*. *Doing what you know* is a completely different thing altogether. And what you'll find this afternoon during the practice sessions is that occasionally you'll slip back into the old language patterns of *you should do, you need to, you ought to, you have to, you must*. Incidentally, we have a name for people who use this kind of aggressive language, especially the 'should-ers' and 'must-ers'. We call them must-debators or mustabators. And you don't want people to think you're a mustabator, do you?

(Laughter.)

It's really important to remember to forget all those judgemental language patterns you don't need anymore. You've been using that language for long enough. You've used up your go, let someone else have a turn at being judgemental!

Got it? Learning embedded? Good, let's move on.

30

language patterns that hinder coaching

NDK. We're going to investigate learning. Listen up. *Words have the power to build up or knock down.* In the coaching situation, we can use language to cause great damage, or we can use words that empower people and make them feel good, that give them more choice and more opportunity. We would guide you towards the second of those two options.

Let's have a look at a number of phrases that can cause damage in the coaching process. This thing here *(draws a But Monster)*, aaarghh! Looks pretty scary doesn't it? This is the But Monster™. This is how it works. "OK, Siobhan, you've made one or two contributions today that have been quite useful. Some of the things you had to say were… good…"

What's coming?

Siobhan. A 'But'!

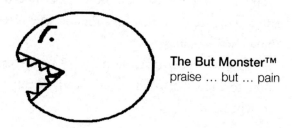

The But Monster™
praise ... but ... pain

NDK. Wow! How did you know that? That's incredible. You must be able to read my mind, or something. Are you a wizard or a shaman of some kind? How did you do that?

(Laughter.)

Siobhan. By your tone.

NDK. By my tone? What *specifically* about my tone did you notice?

Martin. There were some Mars Bars in there.

NDK. There were some Mars Bars in there, yes. Anything else?

Crystal. There was a delay.

NDK. There was a delay, yes.

Dawn. It sort of trailed off.

NDK. Yes, it trailed off. There was something called sentence dropping... there's usually a downward inflection in the voice and a sentence drop that tells the message receiver that something else is coming.

Now, we know that Martin is 23 or thereabouts, and I'm going to guess that you're in your early twenties, at least, Dawn – maybe 21 or 22?

(Laughter.)

Dawn. I wish!

NDK. Now, have you always spoken English? Is that your first language?

Dawn. Yes.

NDK. OK. And were you brought up in a family or a community where English was the first language?

Dawn. Yes.

NDK. OK. That's not always the case; for many people in the UK these days English is not their first language. We have a wonderfully diverse nation. So, for 21 years you've been using English as your chosen language. Now, what happens when you use a language is that after a few years you begin to notice a few trends. You begin to notice after a while that when somebody speaks in that certain way, the chances are that there is a 'But' coming, would you agree?

Dawn. Yes.

NDK. So, after 21 years you know that when somebody says, "Well, you know, you've said one or two useful things today, and some of your contributions have been quite helpful..." with a trail off and downward inflection... and sentence... dro - pp - ing... You make a quick mental and linguistic calculation and you think... hmmm... there's a very good chance that the next word is going to be a...

Several. 'But'!

NDK. That's right. Now, what happens to you as you're waiting for that 'But'?

Sarah. You think you know the 'But' is coming so you anticipate what's coming next.

NDK. Anticipate what?

Sarah. A KITA?

NDK. OK, so what's coming after the 'But' is going to be a KITA or something painful, is that right?

Sarah. Yes.

NDK. What's coming is pain. You know something is coming. Now, incidentally... what happens inside you when you're getting ready for pain?

Crystal. You tense.

NDK. You do what?

Crystal. You tense.

NDK. Did you see that? Did you see what she did when she said that? *(Mimics Crystal's neck tension and shoulder raising.)* She went like that *(tense posture)* when she tensed up. Why did she go like that?

Jack. She was being defensive.

NDK. Defensive. So, how does that *(tense posture)* help?

Sarah. You're getting ready for the kick.

NDK. Getting ready for the kick! You know, we're just mammals, that's all we are. When you think back to the sabre-toothed tiger days, guess what? Well, we had a few choices didn't we? One was what?

Nuj. Fight or flight.

NDK. That's right. Ruunnnn! Or stay and fight. There's a third one though, do you know what it is?

(Silence.)

NDK. Play dead. Freeze. We stay perfectly still and pretend we're not there. It worked really well when we were hiding from prehistoric creatures. Ever experienced that at work when the boss is on the rampage? Think about that for a moment... OK so what we do is get ready, and we're still, millions of years later, doing the same thing, we're *(mimics tension around shoulders)* doing that.

Crystal. Did I really do that?

NDK. You did *(mimics tension around shoulders)*. And probably even worse that that!

(Laughter.)

NDK. So, 21 years old, 21 years of listening to all these language patterns, you know that the chances are that there's a 'But' coming. Not only do you know that, you also know that there's some pain coming, so what do you do, you *(mimics tension around shoulders)* go like that. And that's all because I was about to say 'But'. *(Long pause.)*

So let's think about syntax, about this process. I make some meaningless, trivial platitude about how you've done something reasonably well, with a downward inflection at the end of the statement, and a sentence drop as it trails away. You know that a But Monster™ is coming to bite you, you get ready for some pain, and guess what? *(Pause.)* There is some.

Why are we mentioning this? The reason I mention it is because you can break the spell. You can break the rapport with your coachee – all the lovely cuddly supportive stuff that we created in that coaching session with Jenny – just by using poor tonality and the But Monster. My guidance to you is please find a different way. There are two ways of avoiding using the But Monster, which, by the way, is stuck in your habit. You consistently use this, and until a few moments ago you didn't even know that you used it.

Two other ways... one is, we change the But Monster and just use the word 'And'. Instead of using a downward inflection, we keep it pretty flat or even give a slight uplift at the end of the sentence. We concentrate on the positive. And then, instead of a 'pain' message we offer 'change'... or 'difference'.

And it will go like this... and I'm hamming it up Martin, OK?

(Laughter.)

"Dawn, some of the stuff you said this morning was great! You know, a couple of the comments you made were *really* helpful for the group, and do you know what would be fab for the rest of the day is if you could continue to do those things because it just adds so much value! Are you up for that?"

Dawn. Definitely.

NDK. Excellent!
Different to the But Monster approach?

(Nods from delegates.)

NDK. Here's the second way of avoiding the dangerous But Monster... this is really sneaky. We're good at sneaky. Instead of

'But', a full stop, deep breath, swallow. And of course, no downward inflection or sentence dropping. None of that stuff. What do you mean Nick? Fear not, dear friends, I will explain.

It goes like this... "Sarah, some of the stuff you said this morning was great! You know, a couple of the comments you made were *really* helpful for the group." Full stop, deep breath, swallow. "What would be fab for the rest of the day is if you could continue to do those things because it just adds so much value! Are you up for that?"

Sarah. Yes.

NDK. Excellent!

So, But Monster... we can either cause huge pain – anticipated pain – and break the spell, or we can use and 'And' or we can use a full stop. You got it? Learnt? Is it in your brain? Good, now all you have to do is use these skills. Because knowing what to do is not the same as...

Several. Doing what you know!

NDK. What a talented group you are.

What will happen now – during breaks today, for the rest of the day, for the next few weeks, and for the rest of your lives – is that you will become conscious of the But Monster emerging from your voice box and you'll stop it just in time and replace it with an 'And' or a full stop, deep breath and swallow. And you learnt it here folks.

In your practice sessions this afternoon you'll notice that a 'But' is trying to come out and you can suppress it, or even better just change it for one of the two alternative choices you have available to you. You always have choice about how you communicate, folks.

By the way... by the way, 'by the way' means the same as 'incidentally'. If someone says, "By the way," it almost never means, "By the way," it's usually a very significant message they're giving you. John Grinder taught me that. Anyway, by the way, sometimes people will camouflage the But Monster.

(Draws glasses, hat, and beard on But Monster drawing.)

The Disguised But Monster™
praise ... however ... pain

Maybe they've been on a management course of some kind and they've become all sophisticated, you know what I mean?

(Smiles and nodding heads.)

NDK. So they'll disguise their But Monsters with longer words. They'll say, "You know, some of the things you've said this morning have been quite useful... and one or two of your contributions have been helpful... however..." It's just a posh 'But'!

(Laughter.)

NDK. Listen out for posh Buts.

OK, what's the next damaging language pattern on the list, Sean?

Sean. "What you need to do..."

NDK. Oh yes, "What you need to do..." Ok, Nuj, do you remember, by any chance, some of the language I was using with you during your coaching session?

Nuj. Er, yes...'should'.

NDK. 'Should'. What else?

Nuj. 'Need to'.

NDK. Oh yes, 'need to' and other ones: 'ought to', 'have to', 'got to', 'must'. These are the language patterns of bully coaches. These are bully coach techniques. What bully coaches do is they impose their wills, their maps of the territory on other people. It's an ineffective way of creating sustainable change, because it's a KITA approach. It's imposed. The change does not come from within the coachee. It's not personally motivated.

Now, I've been running these types of events for many years. What usually happens at this point is that people nod sagely and say, "Oh, yes, very good, quite right, yes, I agree absolutely." And the person who does that most is usually the biggest boss in the room. And then what happens in the afternoon when we get to practise all these new skills is that the big boss reverts immediately into his or her default operating system, which is to say, "What you need to do," "What you should do," and "What you must do," language. Over the years I've come to really enjoy watching the inevitable unfold!

(Laughter.)

NDK. Sometimes people 'should' all over the coachee. Remember earlier? You don't really want to be thought of as a mustabator, do you?

(Laughter.)

NDK. It's bullyboy tactics. We don't do it.

What's the next one, John, what does it say in your workbook?

John. "How many times have I told you this?"

NDK. "How many times have I told you this?" For goodness sakes John, how many times? Nice and supportive, eh? How do you feel about that John?

John. Not great.

NDK. Folks, here's a fundamental learning point... if you've been doing something for a while and it's not working, do something else! This is a basic tenet of NLP. It's about recognising that some methods work and some methods don't. If the method you're using doesn't work, change the method! If you've told the guy so many times and 'telling him' hasn't worked, you have a few choices – there are always choices ladies and gentlemen – you could sack him, send him on yet another company indoctrination course, accept that's how he performs in his job role, or change the way you're supporting him as his manager. Have you ever thought that maybe it's you who's at fault here? Think about that…

I was working some years ago with a large corporate retailer and I was helping the company's trainers to learn some of this stuff, so that they could train the people in their company without having to engage me every time. I mean, it makes sense; I'm very expensive!

(Laughter.)

NDK. Anyway, I was working with a retail trainer called Harry, a lovely man from Dundee. He was very intense and serious about his training. We were delivering a session about choices and changing strategy when something isn't working.

There's a great analogy about how stupid wasps are. I'd taught Harry the story and he was repeating it to his group of manager delegates as I sat in on the session as support for him. He was telling the group about how on a hot summer's day, sometimes a wasp will get stuck behind a window and will fly up and down the window trying to get out, repeatedly banging into the glass to try and escape. Harry, as planned, was explaining how the wasp was clearly stupid because, as he watched the wasp, it was trying the same strategy of buzzing up and down and banging against the window, time and time again. The metaphor, of course, is that doing the same thing again, that didn't work lots of previous times, is stupid.

Then he made me laugh. He said, "And you get fascinated by what the wasp is doing, and before you know it you're talking to the wasp, telling it how stupid it is, and that you'll open the window for it. Talking to it! And I don't even speak wasp!"

(Laughter.)

NDK. Anyway, "How many times have I told you this?" Yeah, well try another coaching strategy pal, because that one isn't working.

OK, what's next on the list of language patterns that hinder the personal growth of your staff...?

Dawn. "I don't mean to criticise..."

NDK. What's coming next?

Crystal. But!

NDK. How did you know that? Because you're maybe 19 or 20 or something, you haven't been using this English language stuff for long and yet you know what's coming next! Amazing.

(Laughter.)

NDK. How remarkable is this? What have you got there, Jenny?

Jenny. "You could have done much better."

NDK. Oh, lovely, how encouraging. "You could have done much better." How do you feel now, Jenny?

Jenny. Deflated.

NDK. Do you remember being in the fourth form or the third form when you were being told off at school? Only pleasant memories folks, unless you work for the Environ-Mental Health Department of my local council, in which case please enjoy the misery of the bad memories. I had a nest of rats at the bottom of my garden last year and they wouldn't come and deal with them because they said the rats were coming from the road so it was apparently the responsibility of the Highways Department. We had such fun discussing that one. I had to tell them off. They could have done much better. What's next?

Nuj. "With the greatest of respect."

NDK. Oh, yes. What does that mean?

Nuj. It means you have no respect for the other person, whatsoever.

NDK. Very good. I said that to the Environ-Mental people at the council. I said, "Look, with the greatest of respect..."

(Laughter.)

NDK. What's next?

Martin. "If I were you…"

NDK. Yeah, well you're not, so shut up.

(Laughter.)

NDK. This is so patronising, isn't it? "If I were you…" Oh, you pompous bastard! When you use that kind of language that's what goes through people's minds.

So what I'm introducing you to here are the potential damages that can be caused by injudicious use of these language patterns, patterns that some of you have used… *in the past…* to try and create behavioural change. My guidance to you is to avoid these patterns from now on.

I think there is one more damaging pattern in your workbooks…

Daisy. "Why can't you…?"

NDK. Let me take you through, "Why can't you…?"

When we ask people "Why?" we engage in the process of embedding in people why they can't do things. So, if I say to you, "Why can't you do something?" what do you think you're going to do?

Tony. Give a reason.

NDK. Exactly. You'll think of all the reasons why you can't do it. And it reinforces all the reasoning behind that decision you have made, that you can't do it. A little later we'll discover a mechanism for unlocking the thought process and self-talk that resulted in the decision, "I can't..."

So, how does, "Why can't you..." result in this disempowerment? Well, it's all down to trans-derivational searching! Yes, that's right, folks, it's time to discuss trans-derivational search methodologies – your favourite subject, right Dawn?

Dawn. Definitely. I think.

(Laughter.)

NDK. What happens is this. When someone asks you why you can't do something you go into search mode, just as if you were searching through your computer files looking for a Word doc. You search through the filing cabinets in the brain until you find the Word doc that says, 'that thing I can't do'. You click on it and open the document. And guess what? In the doc is a list of all the reasons why you can't do that thing. Maybe the file name is 'why I can't talk to large audiences'. You've maybe decided that you can't give presentations to large groups. Someone, maybe a colleague, gives you the opportunity to give a talk to a few hundred people. You already know you can't do it because you've *decided* you can't. You say to your colleague, "I'm sorry, I just can't do that. I can't talk to large audiences." And the colleague says, "Why not?" What's coming?

Jenny. All the reasons why you can't.

NDK. That's right, you search through the filing cabinets of your mind and find all the reasons why you can't talk to large audiences. What might the reasons be?

Tony. You've never done it before.

Sara. You did it before and it went wrong.

Crystal. You get a dry throat.

Nuj. You're worried that you'll forget what to say.

John. It makes you feel sick.

Dawn. You don't know your subject well enough.

Nuj. If you screw up, your career will be damaged.

Colin. People will laugh at you.

NDK. Excellent. These are all written down in the Word doc headed 'why I can't talk to large audiences' and can be found in the filing cabinet in your head. What happens is that when you're asked the question, "Why can't you...?" you have some excellent prepared answers, all neatly filed away in your mind. And what's great is you can really reinforce your negative beliefs by repeating the message to the person asking you, and more significantly, to yourself.

"Why can't you...?" is a great way to embed limiting and restrictive belief systems. So, if you really want to reinforce the limitations of your people, find something they've done wrong and start using, "Why can't you...?" much more frequently with your staff. They'll soon get the hang of why they're so rubbish at everything!

(Laughter.)

NDK. Hey, the trans-derivational search idea is just an idea and it might not be scientifically valid, but it's true. And you know that it is, don't you?

(Nods from delegates.)

NDK. OK, so those are language patterns that hinder the effective coaching of your people. We're not going to use those patterns ever again, Daisy, are we?

Daisy. Never.

NDK. Good.

31
constructive language patterns

NDK. Let's have a look at some language systems that work really effectively at creating behavioural change in people.

OK, so what we are up to now, is this. We're suggesting to you that there are a few groups of phrases that can help you enormously in the coaching context. We know that tell, tell, tell doesn't work, don't we?

(Nods from delegates.)

NDK. Let's have a look at three different types of patterns that help build capacity. The first one is 'opening lines'. By now, you'll know that the opening question after we have shown the mystery shopping film is what?

Tony. What did you think?

NDK. That's right, "Well, what did you think?" with no tonal inflection to suggest pleasure or displeasure. It's a very powerful question because it's so open; it allows people to select whatever emotional thought they've got.

"How do you think that went?" is a variation of the same question. There are several opening lines described in your workbook that can stimulate discussion. Now, I mentioned earlier, what will happen is this: when you ask someone the question, "Well, what did you think?" they will go into beat-yourself-up mode and major self-flagellation, "Oh I was terrible, that was awful, I can't believe how bad I was."

Once in a while you'll find someone who flips the picture over and he or she will tell you how perfect he or she is. It's rare, but it does happen occasionally. It happens very, very infrequently. There's a car salesman in Godalming who is apparently perfect. Perfect Peter. His sales manager doesn't think he's perfect, his dealer principal doesn't think so and his sales figures don't support his belief that he's as good as he could ever be, but hey, as long as he's happy...

(Laughter.)

Most of the time people beat themselves up. And remember what I said? We can continue to kick them when they're down, give them a real good KITA kicking, or we can help them to feel better. Our mission is to help people feel good before we get into helping them to become... *(raises arm up and to the left)*...

Several. Even better.

NDK. Very good.

So, "What were you really pleased with?" "What did you really like?" "What were you happy with?" "What went well, do you think?" These kinds of questions are great questions to help folk to start to feel good about themselves. To have a strong ego. And at first the coachee will probably say to you, "Nuthin." But don't give up here, this is where you've got to really power through it. Keep plugging away, "There must have been something, John, you were pleased with? There must have been something? Maybe it was something little? What was it?" Eventually he or she will come out with something, and it will probably be something quite trivial. Grab it for all you're worth and hang on to it!

What we do then is get into something we call a 'yes set'. We get the person to think of more things he or she was pleased with. "What else were you pleased with? Really? Yeah, you're right, that was fantastic, wasn't it! And what else? And what else? And what else?" We call it the 'yes set' because we want people to get into the habit of thinking of other things that they were really pleased with. "And what else were you really pleased with Jenny? And what else, Dawn? And what else, Tony?" until we've got maybe half a dozen things, if we can, that the coachee was really pleased with. Frankly, it's not the end of the world if the things he or she was pleased with are not great in the overall scheme of world events. As long as we get out of people some stuff that they were pleased with and we start to get them to feel good about themselves.

It's at that point that we can start with the next question, "You said earlier that there were a couple of things you would have liked to have done differently? What were they?" Because now that the coachee is feeling good about the things he or she was pleased with, it becomes much less threatening to explore how he or she could have performed differently, or maybe *even better*. Get the idea?

(Nods from delegates.)

NDK. Sometimes in the coaching process people will get stuck. They'll get into that language pattern of, "I don't know." "What were you really pleased with?" "I don't know." "What did you think you did well?" "I don't know." There's an unlocking device we can use to help us, and the coachee, in these situations. It goes like this, "I know you say you don't know what you were really pleased with, but if you did know, what would you say went well?" "Uh?" is the usual response. It sort of scrambles the brain, but it works. And once we have one thing the coachee is pleased with we can get the momentum going with the 'yes set' and really build up a nice list of things.

So these *(refers to workbook)* are prompts. Our guidance to you is to keep this list close at hand at all times when coaching. At first certainly, this reference document will help you, especially if you find yourself or the coachee getting stuck. This afternoon you can use this document, and use it whenever you're conducting a coaching session, at least to begin with.

These questions in the middle here stimulate discussion.

"I noticed that one of the things you did on the film there was to...", "One of the things you said to the customer was..."

On the odd occasion where you do get a resistant coachee, those questions at the bottom are particularly powerful. Encourage and challenge. When you get somebody who's stuck, or who's perfect – and it happens very infrequently - you can use these questions to encourage and challenge. Do you remember the coaching session with Sarah? There was no challenge.

(Shaking heads.)

NDK. Coaching is not just about helping people at work feel good, it's about helping them to stretch themselves, to go beyond their current levels of performance and to extend their capabilities. To do that, it helps if we encourage them to venture outside their current comfort areas to enter the 'stretch zone'.

This is what happens, isn't it? People live and work within their zones of comfort and rarely venture beyond into the scary world of 'new', because it's uncomfortable and possibly dangerous. Who knows, maybe we might find that we're incompetent at something, and how would that feel? Ugh! Obviously nobody in this room has restrictive thinking like that, but some people do.

(Laughter.)

NDK. These questions are very powerful. "I wonder, is there anything that you could have done slightly differently, Sarah?" "Next time you do this Jenny, if you were doing it again, how would you go about it differently?" Notice there is no direct criticism, but just enough implication to suggest that the coachee might want to consider other choices. This is an important point in the coaching process. We are helping the coachee understand that he or she has choice.

People who are stuck in any form of behaviour, and especially in a cycle of mediocrity, often remain there because they have constructed a belief system of limited choice. In terms of

behaviour, they believe that theirs is the only viable way of operating. Your job as a good coach is to help them explore for themselves and discover that there are in fact, a number of
behavioural choices available to them! And that means more
than one choice, ladies and gentlemen. Two choices, for example, is not a choice, it's a dilemma.

(Laughter.)

NDK. So, three sets of questions, opening lines to get conversation going, prompt comments and questions to keep it
moving, and challenge questions to ensure a stretch and to deal
with any 'perfect Peters'. Got it? Embedded in your minds?

Several. Yes.

NDK. Good.

32

can't to can™
change model

NDK. What you are about to learn is the single most powerful language tool you are ever going to come across. At least, that is, until the next most powerful language tool, a bit later on.

(Laughter.)

NDK. Occasionally, people get stuck in their thinking, don't they? They get into what I call a Linguistic Cul-de-Sac™ or a Thinking No-Through-Road™, a kind of thinking block where there's apparently nowhere to go. When people say, "I can't," sometimes it doesn't matter what we say, they seem determined to stay stuck in, *"I can't."* It's almost as though the more we ask, the more determined they are to stick by their statements. They become entrenched.

What sort of 'I can't' thinking do you get from your customer-facing staff?

Dawn. "I can't up-sell warranties."

Martin. "I can't do admin."

Nuj. "I can't deal with aggressive customers."

Sarah. "I can't use the new software."

Daisy. "I can't ask good questions."

Colin. "I can't sell finance."

Nuj. "I can't close the sale."

Tony. "I can't stand my colleagues."

(Laughter.)

NDK. Nice one! Would you be interested in learning a linguistic technique that will help people to move out of 'I can't' towards 'I can'?

Several. Yes!

NDK. I thought so. Well, this is how we do it. Pay attention.

This is called the Can't to Can™ model. I developed it some years ago when I was meeting an awful lot of people who seemed stuck in 'I can't'. They had made their minds up and where not going to be shifted. Do you remember the dangerous 'Why?' question?

Jenny. "Why can't you?"

NDK. That's right, well done. The more I asked these people why they couldn't do something, the more they became entrenched in their own worlds of negativity. The poor souls. I stumbled across a couple of questions I'd discovered from a particular branch of linguistics that you don't even need to know about, and began to recognise how these questions could be used in a commercial context. I had to reshape them a bit, and place them in a structured model. That's what we have here in the Can't to Can model.

Let's explore how it works. Is there anybody here who has yet to pass their driving test? Everyone has passed their test? Fabulous! What I'd like you to do is pretend. Pretend that you can't drive, OK? Let's run through this model. This is a fantastic change model. There are a couple of key parts to it that I'll run through with you in a moment. The limiting belief is, "I can't..."

Colin. I can't drive.

NDK. OK. What we could do now, of course, is to ask which awful question?

Chris. "Why can't you drive?"

NDK. Very good. And we know what happens when people are asked why they can't do something?

NDK. They search through their minds to find a reason that justifies why they can't do it.

Tony. Trans-derivational searching!

NDK. Oh, what a superb delegate! Can you come on all my courses, Tony?

(Laughter.)

NDK. Yes, that's right; people seek out a justifiable reason why they can't do something so they can prove they were right to say, "I can't." In fact, some people would rather be right than happy, ever noticed that? So, asking someone why he or she can't do something is a very poor strategy for creating change. It's a strategy employed by fools. People have asked you this question for years, haven't they? Some of them meant well, and they loved you very much; it's just that they didn't know what they were doing, that's all.

Here's the first question. We call this a freedom question, because the only possible answer to the question is a positive one. And the question is, "What would happen, Jack, if you could drive?" Remember; pretend that you can't!

Jack. I'd have independence.

NDK. Good. What else. Think 'benefit'.

Jack. I'd be able to go to lots of places I've not been to before.

NDK. Oh, right, what else?

Jack. I could take my girlfriend out in the car.

NDK. Excellent. Help Jack out, what else?

John. Get a better job?

Daisy. Go shopping in the car rather than on the bus.

NDK. Very good.

Chris. Go to the beach.

Colin. Go out when you want to.

NDK. Excellent. A whole pile of things, would you agree?

(Nods from delegates.)

NDK. Now this next question is what's called the 'Simpsons question', "Would you like that?"

Several. Yes.

NDK. We call it the Simpsons question because the answer is, "Doh! Of course I would like that." In more stuffy circles it might be called a leading question, but you wouldn't remember it like that so we'll stick to the Simpsons question, "Doh!" Got it?

(Nods from delegates.)

NDK. Now it's time for the second freedom question. This is at the heart of this model. We ask this question a number of times; such is its importance. "What would have to happen to make that happen?" is the full question. So, let's continue with the example we've got, "I can't drive." "What would happen if you could?" "I'd have independence, I'd be able to go to the beach, I could take my girlfriend out," and so on. "Would you like that?" "Doh! Yes, of course I would."

"What would have to happen to make that happen?"

Jack. I'd have to pass my driving test.

NDK. You'd have to pass your driving test. OK, incidentally that was a wonderful answer; it was *really* helpful. What we do now is we continue with the same freedom question until we get down to some specific action. So, Siobhan, you'd have to pass your test. What would have to happen to make *that* happen?

Siobhan. I'd have to take lessons.

NDK. What would have to happen, Chris, for you to take lessons?

Chris. I'd have to get a provisional licence.

NDK. What would have to happen for you to get a provisional licence, Jenny?

Jenny. I'd have to go to the Post Office to get a form.

NDK. The next question is a time ordinal question, "When are you going to do that?" Now in answer to this question we often get 'soon' as a response. We don't want 'soon', we want to use that other word, the important one beginning with 's'. Can you remember what it was?

Dawn. Specifically.

NDK. Good. So, when *specifically* are you going to go and get the form?

Dawn. Now!

NDK. Now? You can't go yet, we've got a training course to run!

(Laughter.)

NDK. So let me just summarise this, can I? You said, Dawn, that if you go to the Post Office now and pick up a form to get your provisional driving licence, you'll be able to get some lessons, which means that you'll be able to pass your test, which means that you'll be able to buy a car, which means that you'll be able to do all those things like going to the beach, having your independence and taking me to the pub, is that correct?

(Laughter.)

Dawn. Yes!

NDK. Thank you. So, we have now moved from a place that says, "I can't do that thing," to a place that says, "If I undertake those activities I said I would do, I will be able to do that thing after all." Now, what I recommend you do is this... this is commitment time. I'm big on this. The plan is fine, but it hasn't created closure yet. It hasn't created a real action plan because it hasn't established commitment. And commitment is, "Doing the thing you said you would do, long after the mood you said it in has left you." Like never drinking again, never smoking again, eating healthily from now on, and all those other things you said you would do when the mood was in you!

(Laughter.)

NDK. So, when you're using the Can't to Can model, this is where I like to get a little bit of direct eye contact for the commitment phase. This is the bit where I'll say, "Now, Tony, this action plan that we've got here... you said you're going to go and do all these things. Are you serious about this or just messing about? *(Direct and intense eye contact with Tony.)*

Tony. I'm serious Nick. Absolutely serious.

NDK. Good, because Tony, I'm going to help you. I'm going to do everything I can to make this happen for you. Are you up for that?

Tony. Definitely.

NDK. Good. Let's achieve this together.

OK, so there's just a little bit of direct eyeball contact involved to gain commitment; just enough for the coachee to know that you're taking this very seriously.

Let's apply this now to your workplace and the kinds of 'I can'ts' you get in reality.

Daisy. I can't sell warranties.

NDK. You can't sell warranties? Oh, OK, let's try that one. We could ask that crappy question, couldn't we?

Sarah. "Why can't you sell warranties?"

NDK. Well funny you should ask that question! Let me have a think... I can't sell warranties because... because what?

Sarah. Because of all the reasons you've used to justify yourself with over the years.

NDK. Exactly. So, let's go through the model. What would happen if you could sell warranties, Daisy? What would be the benefits?

Daisy. I'd make more money. And I'd get you off my back.

NDK. Would you like that?

Daisy. Doh! Yeessss!

NDK. OK, what would have to happen to make that happen, for you to be able to sell more warranties?

Daisy. I'd have to feel more confident about it.

NDK. More confident, eh? Folks, we hear this a lot when we use Can't to Can. In retail, service centres, call centres, and in sales environments, confidence is a key factor in performance excellence. Confidence is a function of knowledge – always has been, always will be. When you're lacking in knowledge about a given activity, it's normal and natural that you should be lacking in confidence when asked to deliver the activity. This is excellent news! It means that it's normal to be lacking in confidence when you don't understand something. It means you don't have to spend hours on a therapist's couch with dribble dripping down off your chin. You're normal! Hooray!

(Laughter.)

NDK. Warranties. This is a great example. We can run through this using the Can't to Can model really well. So, what would have to happen to make you feel more confident, Daisy?

Daisy. I'd need some training.

NDK. Oh, OK. Well, what would have to happen for you to get some training?

Daisy. I'd need to get some help from somebody – probably Jack, because he's good at selling warranties.

NDK. OK, and what would have to happen for you to be trained by Jack?

Daisy. I'd have to ask him.

NDK. Good. So when are you going to ask him?

Daisy. Soon.

NDK. When *specifically?*

Daisy. Tomorrow, when he's in.

NDK. What time tomorrow?

Daisy. As soon as he comes in at nine.

NDK. Good. Lets run through this and make sure I've got this right, Daisy... if you see Jack tomorrow morning at nine when he comes in and arrange a training session with him about warranty product knowledge to help you better understand how warranties work, then you'll get the product knowledge you need, and you'll then be able to sell more warranties. That will mean more money for you and it will get me off your back, is that all correct?

Daisy. Spot on.

NDK. Now, Daisy, are you serious about this or are you just messing about?

really not that bothered about. I can't concentrate for five hours of high-street shopping, and I really don't want to either.

Find somebody you haven't worked with before, go up to them and say, "I like the look of you," and get on with the practising, because as you know folks, "Knowing what to do, is not the same as…?"

Several. "…doing what you know."

NDK. What a great group!

33

behaviour breeds behaviour

NDK. Let's talk about you. When you are acting as coach, your behaviour will impact on the coachee. That's a fact. Behaviour breeds behaviour. And culture starts at the top. For many of you today, you are at the top of your local fiefdom, and your behaviour will influence the culture of your local organisation. People are influenced by their line managers and they tend to replicate.

In a coaching situation, we want the coach to behave in a very positive, upbeat and constructive way. We've already talked about how we want to help people to become even better *(raises left arm up and to the left)*, and we want to strengthen their egos. So, it helps if we get into the right *state* . Do you know what I mean by *state?* The right *state* of mind. We sometimes say this, don't we, "I'm not in the right state of mind," or "I'm in a right old state." Well, if you're going to coach effectively, it's really important that you're in the right state.

What we want to illustrate here is – it's a little bit of fun and games – to illustrate how some of these *states* are less helpful.

Incidentally, the phrase *less helpful* is an interesting one. A long time ago, just after the Berlin Wall came down, I was working in Poland with a group of former Soviet Bloc managers. I was helping them to work in a free-market economy and teaching them the basics of marketing and how to compete commercially. My contact from Poznan was a young man by the name of Marius Tomasciewski. Marius was a real entrepreneur, a young man who is now probably a captain of Polish industry. Anyway, Marius was describing the managers I was due to meet the following day. I asked him about their English, because at that time my Polish was non-existent. Marius taught me a language pattern that I still use to today. He was the master of positivity and understatement. He said that some of the local managers' English was *good* and some was *less good*. I found out the next morning that *good* meant they could just about say hello in English, whereas *less good* meant completely blank faces all day. I decided to learn some Polish. *Less helpful* reminds me of Marius and his positive language patterns.

Some of the behaviours we are about to explore are *less helpful* in coaching people to new levels of performance.

Let's have at look at the first one – it's called PLOM. I need you to stand up folks, if you would please?

(Everyone stands.)

NDK. You'll need a little space, that's right. You're about to experience PLOMism. I need you to stand with your feet shoulder-width apart; depending how wide your shoulders are, that will dictate how wide apart your feet should be. Bend your knees. I want you to lean your shoulders forward, and make your chest concave so that the diaphragm is smaller than it would be normally. I want you to drop your arms forward and then drop your head right down so that you're looking down, and right, looking at your right foot. And as you do that I want you to heave a big sigh. And now *(quiet, slow, monotone voice)* I want you to tell me how fantastic the coaching session you're going to deliver will be, after lunch. Repeat after me, *(still quiet, slow, monotone voice)* "I'm going to deliver a fantastic coaching session after lunch." Stay in this posture. Ready? Here we go...

(Everyone in PLOM posture, with quiet slow monotone voices.) "I'm going to deliver a fantastic coaching session after lunch."

NDK. OK! Shoulders up, chin up, eyebrows up, arms back, deep breath, in through the nose, fill the lungs right up – when you're full, exhale through the mouth. *(Raises voice.)* Stretch the muscles around your eyes and mouth, shake off your arms and legs and now try and be depressed! Notice how much better you feel already. Well done everyone, you've just experienced PLOMism; PLOM meaning Poor Little Old Me. You can sit down now.

Have you met any PLOMs at work?

(Nods from delegates.)

NDK. Ever been a bit PLOMmy yourself?

(A few nods.)

NDK. It's an awful thing, PLOMism. Incidentally, you can spot a PLOM really easily. They are the people who come into work in the morning in the PLOM posture. (*Illustrates the PLOM posture again.*)

When you ask them, "Hey! How's it going?" they will usually say something like, *(slow ponderous PLOM voice, still in PLOM posture)* "Not <u>too</u> bad."

Ladies and gentlemen, you have my explicit authority to be ruthless with PLOMs. Why? Because PLOMism is contagious. It will infect your business like a virus. Misery loves company and the PLOMs are just looking for someone to feel sorry for them.

When they say, "Not *too* bad," you have my personal authority to ask them, "Oh yeah? Well just how fucking bad is it then?"

(Some laughter, but mostly shocked faces.)

NDK. If you are a PLOM in your role as a coach, what do you think that's doing to your coachee? Behaviour breeds behaviour, people, and if you're operating out of PLOM get ready, because you're about to create a team *full* of PLOMs. Get the idea?

(Nods from delegates.)

NDK. Good. No more PLOMism.

OK, the next strategy that we'd ask you to avoid, as a coach, is what we call Ah-Buts. Ah-Buts are the kind of people who – whenever there's a new proposal, or a new strategy put in place, or a new personal action plan – they will say, "Ah, but…this is the reason why it won't work." Bless them! They make rubbish coaches. Don't do it.

What's next, Sean?

Sean. CAVE People.

NDK. CAVE people are from the same family as the Ah-Buts. They are Continuously Against Virtually Everything. Any coach who is Continuously Against Virtually Everything has a challenge on his or her hands when it comes to helping other people strive for new levels of performance, or helping them compete in new fields of endeavour. Where's the integrity? Ever met any CAVE people?

Sarah. Oh yes!

NDK. CAVE people make rubbish coaches. And they lack integrity.

What else have we got, Jenny?

Jenny. ICBAs.

ICBAs. Any ideas folks?

John. I Can't Be Arsed.

NDK. Very good. If you've got a coach operating in I Can't Be Arsed mode, well... behaviour breeds behaviour. And guess what you're going to get from the coachee if you're in I Can't Be Arsed mode?

Several. They can't be arsed.

NDK. Correct, they can't be arsed either.

Next one, Nuj?

Nuj. Deborah Dyson and the Psychic Vampires.

NDK. It's not a rock band. This is a subspecies from the family of creatures known as the Mood Hoovers.

(Laughter.)

NDK. These are folk who come into the room and suck all the energy and goodness out. And if you're a coach operating as a Mood Hoover you've got a challenge. One of my colleagues used to refer to what he called 'a nice cup of tea moment'. It's that time in the morning when you've come in to work and you haven't decided yet whether it's going to be a good day, or a great day. You haven't decided yet. And then the Mood Hoover comes in – sometimes he or she is Psychic Vampire – and he or she just sinks those old teeth into the jugular of everybody in the room and sucks out all the energy and positivity from your veins. Have you met those folk before?

(Nods from delegates.)

NDK. Obviously there's nobody in this room who is a Mood Hoover.

(Laughter.)

NDK. Behaviour breeds behaviour. If you're a coach operating as a Psychic Vampire, a Mood Hoover or a Deborah Dyson, then get ready for low performance returns on your coaching activity, because you're not going to be very successful.

I used to call Deborah Dyson 'Deirdre Dyson' until I was explaining Mood Hoovers one day to a lucrative new client, and guess what her name was? Deirdre. I thought it commercially prudent to change the name. That works fine until the next big client opportunity comes along with Deborah as the decision maker. I need to do some thinking about that.

What's the next one? What have you got on the list, Martin?

Martin. MGs.

NDK. MGs. Moaners and Groaners. Closely related to BMWs: that's Bastards, Moaners and Whingers. Not ideal attributes for a positive and inspirational coach.

What else have we got. Daisy?

Daisy. 20/20s.

NDK. 20/20s. These are those folk who say, "Look, I don't need to learn anything new, I'm the finished article, I've been doing this kind of work for 20 years." We call them 20/20s because what we find is this: they haven't actually got 20 years' experience, they actually have one year of experience replicated in exactly the same way, 20 times.

(Laughter.)

NDK. They have the same operating style, the same thinking process, the same mindset. It has never changed, and it's not likely to, either, no matter what you say. Have you met any 20/20s?

(Nods from delegates.)

NDK. 20/20s make dreadful coaches because they're so set in their ways, they're not open to change and they feel threatened by any suggestion that they could operate in a different way. They are resistant to change. They are resistant to new ways of thinking. How do you think that fits with the culture of continuous improvement that coaching strives to achieve? It doesn't, so 20/20 behaviour is *less helpful* when it comes to coaching. But nobody in this room, eh? Phew!

I had a client recently who said, "Nick, we don't have any 20/20s." I said, "Well that's great, you're a very fortunate organisation." He said, "No we're not, we're full of 30/30s!" Oh dear.

(Laughter.)

NDK. That was an organisation where people are there a *long* time.

Tony. How are 20/20s different to CAVE people?

NDK. 20/20s are long-serving employees, or maybe people who've been in the industry a long time. CAVE people may be new to the business and still Continuously Against Virtually

Everything. That's a recruitment issue, I'd argue.

Dawn, what else have we got?

Dawn. Bus Drivers and Passengers.

NDK. Bus Drivers and Passengers. This is a great one for you fine folk, as well as the coachee. This is about who is in charge of your destiny. Are you driving the bus, or are you a passenger on somebody else's bus? Are you sub-contracting your life out to somebody else, or are you deciding what you want to do? Your choice. Whether you're a coach or a coachee, who is at the front driving your bus? Is it you? Or are you sitting at the back, going wherever you're taken?

Jack, what else have we got?

Jack. EGGs.

NDK. We love EGGs! EGGs are the kind of positive people who make fabulous coaches. EGGs know that with the right plan, and the right commitment, people can achieve amazing things. EGGs know that Everything is Going Great – now listen carefully... and if it's not, *it soon will be* if we put some dedicated effort in to change things round. They are inspirational people who get the best out of their coachees by being positive and solution-focused.

These types of coaches frame the world in a positive way. They see all the opportunities and possibilities in the universe today! They make you believe that things are possible. If the input is right, then an output will come. They're not reckless dreamers, though. They know that there has to be application

Daisy. I'm very serious about it.

NDK. Excellent, because Daisy, I'm going to do everything I can to support you on this.

Got it everybody? It's so easy. At the heart of it are those two freedom questions. Powerful stuff.

Now, a note of warning. Sometimes the coachee will come up with a number of things that 'have to happen to make it happen'. This can be problematic. The model works really well by drilling down into one activity at a time. For example, recently a manager working with the model explained that a number of things had to happen in order for his coachee to be able to move forward. This is fine. What we need to do in such circumstances is to address each required activity as a stand-alone item.

Can't to Can works well on one front at a time. Take the 'I can't drive' example from earlier. After the question, "What would have to happen for you to be able to drive a car?" Dawn could reasonably have said, "I need lessons and I need to buy a car."

We can deal with the lessons issue and then subsequently we can deal with the buying a car issue, but not at the same time, OK? So, be careful when somebody comes up with a personal strategy that says, "I need to do this, and this, and this, and this." A key skill for you will be to ensure that you fight on one front at a time when using Can't to Can. OK?

(Nods from delegates.)

NDK. It's practice time! When you practise, make sure you select a limiting belief that you would dearly love to overcome. The model doesn't work if the 'I can't' is something you're and that things might not be fantastic at this very moment, but Everything will be Going Great if sustained effort is applied.

This is an important point folks, because some of the Neggies you're going to meet, they're going to say, "Well, it's not going great, is it? It's all right you and your positive mental attitude, but the fact is it's not great at all." That's why we have to emphasise that it is possible to change things. EGGs do that. They understand that people have choices, if only they open their eyes and see them. We want coaches who are solution focused, who are goal oriented and who want outcomes. EGGs are not interested in knowing how you got where you are today. They don't care. It's where you go from here that counts. They don't care what's happened in the past. Where do we go from here, that's the real key. Behaviour breeds behaviour and good coaches are solution oriented.

I'm hoping we have a room full of EGGs here today. Can I just check?

(Nods and smiles.)

NDK. Good.

34

coaching
observed
behaviour

NDK. Before we start on how we use mystery shopping in coaching, let me make something clear. The skills and techniques you're learning today *do not* require you to have access to mystery shopping video footage or audio files. Absolutely not necessary.

Everything you're learning on this programme can be used to reflect on the performance of an employee who has recently engaged in a customer-facing activity. You don't need film to do that, but it does help if you've just seen or heard the employee in action. Some of the best coaches I've come across use *observed behaviour* as the reference material they use in coaching. I would recommend that these coaching processes become part of the everyday activity of a good team leader or manager, whether you have mystery shopping materials available or not. Some of the best coaching managers I've seen in action didn't have the luxury of video footage or telephone recordings when they were weaving their magic.

The real stars of what we might call 'everyday coaching' take time out every day to watch and listen to their people interact with others – maybe with customers, or maybe with colleagues – and then meet with the coachee, while the memory of the interaction is still fresh, to conduct the coaching activity.

Let me give you an example. I was supporting a new coach recently in a retail store. Her name was Penny and she was delightful. We were working on her ability to coach her people using visual mystery shopping video footage. While I was with her, we decided to conduct some 'observed behaviour' coaching so that I could help her improve her skills to *even higher* levels. Notice anything in that language?

John. *Even higher.* You're using language patterns that are about you coaching her. You're coaching her in her ability to coach!

NDK. That's right.

What we did was this: we both watched and listened to a member of her team working with a customer in the process of providing a service, and helping the customer to buy a product. By the way, *(pause)* that's so much nicer than 'selling', isn't it?

We both watched the team member and when the interaction was over and the customer had left the store, Penny approached her colleague with a smile and said, "Hey Steph, I was just watching you with that customer, you did some really great things there! Have you got a minute for quick chat? I'd like to congratulate you on some of the specific things you did. We might be able to pick up on an idea or two as well. Fancy a cuppa?"

Steph was up for it and they had a 10-minute chat in the back office with a cup of tea. I sat in as Penny coached Steph and they jointly identified a mini plan to help Steph *continue to* do some things really well, and to *begin to* introduce a technique into Steph's service delivery that was new to her. The discussion was elegantly facilitated by Penny and didn't even seem to be a coaching session in the formal sense. But she'd been on this programme and she knew exactly what she was doing. There was a Structure to her Well-Done-Ness!

Video footage or telephone recordings help enormously, but you don't need them to be able to use these fabulous language patterns that create behavioural change. Happy with that?

(Nods from delegates.)

NDK. Good. Let's get into mystery shopping.

35

coaching using mystery shop recordings

NDK. What we're now going to do will be new to you. We're about to explore a well-proven process for coaching using video film or audio file sourced during a visual or telephone mystery shopping programme. I know it's well proven because I was the first person to develop a framework coaching model to use with mystery shopping materials, and along the way I have made some huge cock-ups. I think the human resource people call this the 'stochastic' method of learning. I call it trial and error with loads of foul-ups that taught me what works and what doesn't.

You're very lucky because you get what works well without the time investment I've put in over the years, or the pain I've endured. Or, more accurately, the pain other people have endured. Some of the mystery shopping coachees I practised on had quite a lot of pain while I was doing my bull in a china shop impressions. I guess there's a cost in any research-and-development programme.

Who is using visual or telephone mystery shopping materials currently? *(Arms raise.)* OK, most leading retail and service sector organisations now use mystery shopping to test the efficacy and quality of the service they offer to customers. It makes sense. To say that recorded mystery shopping film or audio offers a learning and development resource is a statement of the bleedin' obvious.

So, who would be interested in knowing how to use mystery shopping material to coach with elegance and excellence, through a structured and proven process?

Several. Yes please!

NDK. Oh, all right then. Here goes.

You now know some of the skills and linguistic tools we can use in the coaching process. This is about the process steps, rather than the skills or tools.

First things first. Let's assume that the communication process has taken place and that the workforce understand what mystery shopping is and why the organisation is conducting a visual or telephone programme. I guess it could be an email mystery shop programme, too.

We've reached the stage when a visual mystery shop DVD has arrived at your store or dealership, marked for your attention. Gulp! You'll be thinking, "Yikes! Now, what did I learn with Nick? Where are my course notes?"

(Nervous laughter and nods.)

NDK. First up... let's look at preparation. What do want to prepare?

Sean. The room?

Sarah. Yourself. You'll want to get in the right state.

Dawn. Watch the DVD and take notes.

NDK. OK, good. You're going to take a look at that film and take some notes. You'll want to identify the key points in the customer's experience and decide how you feel about what are called the 'moments of truth' for the customer; that is, the points where something significant happened in the customer journey.

Now, you'll have your own customer service processes or sales processes that you expect your people to follow. These make an excellent framework reference for you as you review the DVD prior to the coaching session. The mystery shopping company will have agreed with your organisation a report format that includes the customer-service processes or sales processes that are important to the business. The report will show how the employee featured on the film has performed when measured against these behaviours. It will also include a score as a percentage. Do not reveal the score to the coachee under any circumstances until the coaching session is complete.

Incidentally, we talk about an employee being *featured on film*, rather than *caught* or *captured*. Featured has much more of a Hollywood feel about it, don't you think? Some people like to talk about people being *caught doing it right*. Dreadful! The word caught does all the damage, well before you get to *doing it right*. Stick to *featured*.

You might need to watch the DVD more than once to make sure you've addressed all these points yourself and that you're familiar with the main factors. In fact, I'd encourage you to do that. Sometimes we miss things first time round.

OK, you'll need to print off an action plan for the coachee. The action plan – there's one in your workbook – follows the Continue & Begin approach we described earlier. Just take a look. Can you see? There are a couple of key parts to this that you need to know about. The first is *continue to* and the second is *begin to*. What we do is we work on a ratio of two to one. So, when people have seen themselves featured on film, we encourage them to identify as many things as they can that they'd like to continue to do well. That's why we put so much effort into, "What were you really pleased with?" The two to one ratio means, of course, that if we've identified six things that they'd like to continue to do well, we can justifiably ask for...

Jack. Three things to do better?

Daisy. *Even* better!

Nuj. Differently!

NDK. What a group! Yes, *up to*, not always three; *up to* three things that they might like to begin to do *differently*. Maybe it's only two things, but six and three is pretty much the ideal ratio in my experience of, probably now, *thousands* of coaching sessions. Maybe it's four and two; it depends how much material you have to work with on the DVD or audio file. Never, ever, step beyond the two to one ratio. And why are we doing that? Why do we want twice as many *continue to* behaviours as *begin to?*

Martin. Ego.

NDK. Ego. We want people to feel good.

OK, so lets go back to our flow chart and understand what we do next. 'Print off the evaluation report.' This is the report prepared by your company and the mystery shopping company. The report identifies in very specific language a series of processes and behaviours that the mystery shop programme is designed to measure. There will be, usually, about 20 to 25 questions, sometimes a few less, and occasionally far too many. The questions will be presented in language that allows the measurement process to produce a *yes* or a *no* answer.

Each question has a weighted score to reflect the importance of the behaviour it measures. So, for example, "Was the team member wearing a name badge?" might score only 10 points, whereas, "Did the team member ask at least two questions to understand the customer's needs?" might score 20 points. The points are all added up and an overall percentage is calculated for the mystery shop performance. 50% might be relatively poor, whereas 85% is good. Get it?

(Nods from delegates.)

NDK. Good.

There should never be any potential for answers to be anything other than these two explicit responses, *yes* or *no*. If there is, then the mystery shopping company has not done its job properly. Each question should have what's called a *definition* that describes precisely what is meant by the question so that it's easy to make a judgement on a *yes* or a *no* response.

What works great is if you print off a blank version of this report, with no scores marked against the questions. We can then use this blank report as a reference document during the coaching session without having to divulge the coachee's score against each question. Brilliant!

What we don't want to do is shove the marked report straight under the coachee's nose and say, (*approaches John*) "Hello John, you've been caught on film, and it's not great, you've only scored 35%. We need to have a serious talk."

(Laughter.)

NDK. Remember folks; the score is just a measure of behaviour against a set of pre-determined criteria. It's not the score that needs to *continue to* or *begin to* be different; it's the behaviour. The score reminds people of school and exam marks. How did you feel when you got a mark of 35%? Not great, eh? So it's not the score we need to focus on, it's the behaviours. We can reveal the score at the end of the coaching session when we've covered off the important bit – the employee's compliance with your company's explicit service standards and processes, and the behaviours that support them.

So, we use blank reports in what we call 'yes/no' format. The blank reports give us an opportunity to ask the coachee how he or she thinks he or she did in relation to the behaviours measured by the report questions. It's much more powerful when we ask the coachee what he or she thinks. And you know the first question we ask, don't you?

Jenny. "Well, what did you think?"

NDK. Good. And the likely answer?

Daisy. "I can't believe I was so bad…"

NDK. Usually something like that, yes. Our guidance to you on this thorny issue of the score is to leave it right to the end. The score changes nothing. We use the blank sheet as a means of creating behavioural change. We don't want the coachee to know the score. What happens is that if we say to Colin, "Hey great news, you've scored 100% on the mystery shop!" how receptive is Colin going to be to a performance-improving coaching session?

Daisy. Not very – he'll think he's already perfect.

Sarah. Like the car salesman in Godalming!

NDK. Exactly. And what's important for you to recognise is that no matter how high the score, there is almost always room for improvement. The mystery shop can't test for everything. I've seen some mystery shop films that meet the needs of the report, but there was definitely an opportunity for the featured employee to improve. Some people tick all the boxes but just don't have that warmth we all love as a customer. It's very difficult to measure some personal attributes with a yes/no answer.

How receptive is Colin going to be if he scored 10%?

Jack. Not very.

NDK. Correct. We don't want to get anywhere near the scores folks – nowhere near, OK?

Nuj. We'll need copies of the blank report without scores.

NDK. Yes you will. Lets go back to our flow chart. We've said, "Watch the film and take some notes." Our guidance is, watch the film again and take some more notes. Print off the Continue & Begin action planning sheets, print off the blank report without scores, and plan the coaching session.

Now, let's think about this – the coaching session. I say to Siobhan, "Hi Siobhan, you've been caught on film. Frankly, it wasn't very good and you've got a lot to work on. Now, I'm going on holiday for the next couple of weeks and when I come back I want to see you at 10 o'clock in my office, to deal with this." Gulp! What's happening to Siobhan?

Tony. She's going to be anticipating what you're going to discuss with her.

NDK. Ha! If she's still there when I come back! This is the old trick, isn't it, of the bully boss who gives you bad news on a Friday afternoon so that you have all weekend to worry about it and spoil the weekend for you and your family. Low-life filth and vermin scumbags do that. I've met some. Please don't do that.

What I recommend is to say, "Hey Siobhan, great news! We've had the mystery shop come through and guess what? You're featured on it this time! There's some fab stuff on there.

Get the kettle on, grab a cuppa, let's get together and take a look at it. You up for it?"

Siobhan. Er, yes, OK.

NDK. As quick as you can, as little notice as possible. We don't want the poor woman worrying about it, particularly on the first and second waves of mystery shopping when people are still getting to grips with the whole idea. If we get it known as a positive experience – and we've seen lots of organisations turn it into the most wonderful positive experience – once that's happened a few times, she really will be saying, "Excellent!" But the first few times we need to be extra careful in how we give someone the news that he or she has been featured on a mystery shop film.

Sometimes when a mystery shopping campaign begins, there is lots of anxiety in the air, so please don't make it more threatening than it already appears to some people. Keep the lead-in time short and sweet.

All right, then. Arrange the room and prepare your own state. How are you going to do that? How are you going to arrange the room? Are you going to sit opposite each other with a big desk between the two of you? Maybe you could have a big chair and the coachee could have a little low chair so she remembers who is boss? Maybe sit behind a big table? What do you think?

John. Shoulder to shoulder.

Jack. Ten to two.

NDK. What, no table?

Daisy. No, unless it's a low coffee table.

NDK. OK. Think about these things. Your own state is important. We talked about that earlier. What state of mind are you in for this coaching session? Have you had a bad day, are you thinking, "Right, I'll give him a right kicking"? Are you going to go through the motions? What state of mind are you in? Are you fully prepared? *(Raises voice.)* Are you rushed? Are you stressed? Are you still waiting for that telephone call you're expecting? Let's go through the rest of the session in sequence.

Meet the featured coachee one-to-one. Bring those action plans with you, because you're going to need them!

Build up rapport and reassure. "Siobhan, there's some fab stuff on this DVD, there's some really good stuff. We'll have a look in a second. It's going to be good, enjoy it!"

Briefly explain the process. "What's going to happen Siobhan, is this... we're going to look at the film..." Incidentally, what's going on in her mind right now?

Dawn. Get on with it!

NDK. Quite right! Get on with it! Put the bloody thing in the DVD player and let me see how I did. That's what she's thinking, so let's do that. Put the film in.

Issue the blank report sheet, sometimes called the yes/no sheet. Because what we're going to do is we're going to say to her, "We're going to have a look at the film in a moment. Can you take a quick look at the report so you can see what the mystery shopping company has been asked to measure? Have a look for a while and make yourself familiar. Let's have a look at the kind of things we should be paying attention to as we watch the DVD. As we go through the film, you might like to have a look at the report.

I'll tell you one thing for free, once the film starts they don't even look at the report anymore, they are totally focused on the film. But what we're doing here with the report is, we are introducing them to the Structure of Well-Done-Ness. With me?

(Nods from delegates.)

NDK. We give him or her the yes/no blank report sheet and we show the video. The coachee will say, at some point during that 10 or 15 minutes of film, whatever it is, "Oh, I remember that day, I remember him or her, I remember."

(Nervous laughter.)

NDK. "Oh dear me, that was the night after so-and-so. Oh, look at that, oh, look, there's Lorraine in the background!" What the coachee will do is, he or she will want to engage you in what is happening on the film. Don't get sucked into conversation. Here's my tip to you...

What I could do is engage in conversation, "Oh, really, that's interesting, did you really? Is Lorraine a colleague?" Meanwhile, we're missing what's happening on the film! So, do something that is just slightly rude, would you? Stay focused, intensely, on the film and ignore all comments from the coachee. He or she will soon get the idea that the film is the focus for attention. It may feel a little uncomfortable at first, but stick with it. After all, it's the behaviours we want to address, not what happened on the coachee's night out before the mystery shop. The less you speak to the coachee, the better. That (*points to screen*) is what we're interested in. OK?

(*Nods from delegates.*)

NDK. And then we run the coaching session! And you already know how to do this! What do you do? Turn the film off and say...?

Sarah. "Well, what did you think?"

NDK. "Oh God, I was dreadful! I need to beat myself up. Where's my whip?"

(*Laughter.*)

NDK. "Hey, look, Daisy, I'm sure there are a couple of things you might want to do differently. Let's park those over here for a while (*mimes moving box to side table*). What do you think you did well? What were you really pleased with?"

"Nothing."

"What? Nothing at all? There must be something you thought you did well."

"No."

"Come on, have a think back, what did you do well?"

"Well, I suppose..."

And what they'll do then is they'll come up with something that they think they did OK. Grab it for all you're worth!

Sean. If we're really struggling to find something positive – and knowing what some of my team members are like, some of them will have a negative frame of mind before they even watch the DVD – can we guide them towards something positive? Can we say, "Well, let's have a look at your meet and greet, it went really well."

NDK. Yes you can. We have a wonderful tool to help us do that. What's it called?

Dawn. The yes/no blank report.

NDK. I'd defy anybody to go through all the questions in the report and not find something that the coachee has done well. This is why it's so useful to have the report close at hand. If you do find you're struggling to find something positive, you can go through the yes/no sheet until you find something. Now, you're at a distinct advantage over the coachee in terms of knowledge about his or her performance. Why?

Martin. Because you know the scores.

NDK. That's right. You have the scores against each question, and you've watched the film at least twice, so you know where he or she has done well, and where he or she has done less well. Sometimes you have to nudge. Do you remember the prompt questions? We looked at a series of questions in 'Phrases to Consider'. Do you remember that?

Jack. "I noticed one of the things you did was, X, Y, Z."

NDK. Very good, Jack. Have a Mars Bar.

(Laughter.)

NDK. If you do find the coachee, or you, are stuck, use the prompt questions or use the yes/no sheet and you'll find something positive really quickly. Once you've got one thing you're happy with then you'll very quickly find another. And another.

Nuj. Nick, when does the coachee fill out the yes/no sheet? Or is it the coach?

NDK. The coachee does the writing. In any coaching situation it should always be the coachee who does the writing. We're not actually going to get him or her to go through the yes/no sheet line by line: that would be tedious and very time consuming. We're using it as a support tool, if we need it. What we will do is, when we get to the stage where we say, "Ok, Nuj, what were you really pleased with?" and we get a, "Nothing." that's when we might use it as a means of stimulating discussion. But we don't go through it line by line. The yes/no sheet is very useful for us if and when the coachee gets stuck in negativity or has a blank mind.

You might say, "Let's have a look at some of the questions, shall we?" And what you'll do is you'll say something like, "Look at question seven. 'Did you approach the customer within one minute of her entering the store?' Well, what do you think, coachee?"

You already know that he did because you've got the scored report and you've watched the film at least twice.

And the coachee says, "Yes, I did."

"Yes you did do that, well done, you can put a tick in that box if you want to. What else did you do well? Let's have a look at another question... did you smile when you approached the customer?"

Nuj. Yes, I did.

NDK. Excellent! That's two things you've done well. I suppose you'd like to continue to do those things well in the future, wouldn't you?

Nuj. Of course.

NDK. Great. Even if the initial positive statement is trivial, hang on to it for dear life!

Jenny. Can I just check? Did you say that we give the yes/no sheet to the coachee before he or she starts watching the video?

Yes. As we sit down we say, "Here's a copy of the question set that the mystery shopping company has been asked to measure us on. There's a whole pile of things they have been asked to measure. Let's have a quick scan through and see the sort of things they're measuring. Some of them are environmental, to do with the layout of the store or dealership. Some are to do with the way we approach and communicate with the customer, and some are to do with the service or sales process we're expected to follow in this organisation. The results will show how well the company's training programmes are working." OK, with that?

Nuj. Yes, that's helpful, thanks. I was just wondering if we give them the yes/no sheet if they will concentrate on the blank report – if they'll not be watching the film?

NDK. As soon as that film comes on they lock on to the footage and ignore the yes/no sheet completely. I think it's some kind of default setting of the mind. They get into a deep, deep trance, focusing on the film footage, or the audio file if it's a telephone mystery shop. The reason the yes/no sheet is important is if somebody gets stuck when it's time to identify a positive behaviour.

It happens the other way as well. On the odd occasion that you find yourself working with car salesmen in Godalming, you'll need to ask some of the challenge questions, and the yes/no sheet works well to help you remember some good questions. It's a support tool we use when it's convenient for us to use it. Does that answer your question?

Nuj. Yes, thank you.

Sarah. Is this something you'd introduce before the coaching session to show the kind of things that the mystery shopping programme investigates?

NDK. Not investigate. Listen to the word. What does the word 'investigate' suggest?

Martin. The police. Detectives. Crime!

NDK. Exactly. Be very careful about the words you use, folks. The mystery shopping programme measures some of the environmental factors, processes and behaviours that a customer experiences when he or she comes into our dealership or store. That's it. There's no investigation. We don't need to tie the coachee to a chair and shine a spotlight in his or her eyes, although I've met a few people I'd like to have done that to.

(Laughter.)

OK, so action planning time. The coachee now prepares his or her own action plan.

36

action planning (with mystery shopping)

NDK. You give the Continue & Begin action plan to the coachee, and give him or her a pen, too. This is very important. And you say, "You'd better make a few notes then, about the things you want to continue to do well. What did you say you were really pleased with?"

"Oh, I wore my name badge, I approached the customer within 30 seconds of her coming into the store, I smiled..." whatever it was that the coachee was pleased with, we want him or her to record that on the Continue & Begin action plan.

"OK, let's make sure we capture those good things on *your* action plan. How many have you got now? Five? Brilliant! Now, Sarah, when we turned the film off you said there were a couple of things you wanted to begin to do in a different way. What were those things?" And you only want two or three.

Have any of you been on a safari holiday?

(Blank faces.)

NDK. You've not eaten elephant steak? It's very tasty but you need very big plates!

(Groans.)

NDK. Sorry. You have to cut elephant steak into much smaller slices, and that's what we do with the *begin to* behaviours. There might a hundred things your coachee wants to address, or maybe you think he or she *should* address. We can't do everything at once though, so we choose a small number of *begin to's* and work on them.

I remember one organisation I worked with, a really famous high-street retailer, and the ops director of the business came on this workshop to learn how his branch managers could coach customer-facing employees from observed behaviour *and* from mystery shopping footage. We watched a clip of one guy featured on film and he said there were 16 things that the featured employee *needed to do better, immediately!* I nearly cried.

Sixteen things. Are any of you familiar with seven, plus or minus two?

(Blank faces.)

NDK. OK, George Miller... write this stuff down, or forget it. How soon do you want to start writing this down, Colin? Now, or in a moment?

(Colin smiles and picks up his pen.)

NDK. George Miller identified what he called seven, plus or minus two. He argued that most people can hold, in their conscious minds at any given moment, between five and nine pieces of information. That's seven, plus or minus two. Depending on the circumstances and their innate ability to hold onto random facts, they will hold five, six, seven, eight or nine pieces of information in their conscious minds. Some people can manage more, but Miller reckoned that somewhere in the region of five to nine was normal. Now, if you are seriously asking a coachee to change 16 of his or her behaviours immediately, you're setting yourself and the coachee up for failure, because it ain't gonna happen!

Now, we can easily remember five things, but ask anyone to remember nine or more and we might have to start doing a few memory games.

Of course, people can hold an awful lot of information in their *unconscious* minds, but that comes from practice until it becomes habit, unless you plan on offering direct suggestions or embedded commands through hypnotic trance induction?

(Laughter.)

NDK. So tell people, "I want you to remember 16 things to do differently," and the brain goes into meltdown. It can't cope.

Asking people to take action on more than a few changes is asking for trouble. You're setting the coachee up for failure. Please don't do that. It's far more effective to identify a few key behavioural changes that are manageable and can be implemented with relative ease as the coachee focuses, consciously, on the different approach he or she has committed to. This is the beauty of the Continue & Begin model. It's so simple. Once these new, or different, behaviours become established the coachee can take on other *begin to's*, but not all at once please. In fact, what often happens is that the *begin to's* move to become…

Nuj. *Continue to's?*

NDK. Exactly. And that is the true measure of coaching effectiveness. What happens a few days later is this… as her coach, and probably her line manger, although not always, I can ask Jenny, "Hey Jenny, how are you getting on with those *continue to's* and *begin to's?* And we don't need Jenny to spend hours on the therapist's couch with dribble dripping off her chin as we undertake an archaeological dig into her past.

(Laughter.)

NDK. Don't laugh, that's pretty much what some coaching programmes encourage new coaches to do! God knows what damage is being caused by the psycho-babblers.

And we don't need mystery shopping video footage to conduct a coaching session, either. We can say, "Hey Jenny, I was just watching you with that customer there – I can see you've been working on your action plan already. Got a minute? Let's go through how that went."

And before you know it some of those *begin to's* have become *continue to's*. It's so beautifully simple.

But how does the coachee feel about the coaching session, you may be thinking? This is where you, as coach, can benefit by conducting some professional selling. OK, Sean, you've been featured on the mystery shopping film, how do you feel about that?

Sean. I'm feeling a little bit apprehensive.

NDK. Yes, of course you are, I can understand that. How do you think it went?

Sean. Not bad actually, a lot better than I thought.

NDK. Excellent. And you've got a wonderful action plan there now. Well done! What we're doing here folks is our sales pitch. This is a test for the effectiveness of your coaching prowess. The test for the effectiveness for the coachee is if he or she says, "Yeah, it was good actually," and then you say, "Hey Sean, that is such a cool action plan, you know what would be great would be... if you could share the plan with your teammates, so they can see what's involved when they're featured in a mystery shop. I reckon the rest of the team could learn loads from what we've just done. Would that be OK?"

If you've run the session well, the coachee will say, "Yeah, I'm up for that. That will be all right."

That's the first part of the sale. Now many of you are from a sales background, is that right?

(Nods from delegates.)

NDK. Good, so you'll know that you sometimes sell incrementally; that is, you sell ideas, products, or services bit by bit as the customer becomes more trusting. The same applies here. Once you've got the OK to share the action plan, we can move on to the really important bit – sharing the film or audio file. The same approach applies. Let's keep going with Sean. You could adopt an assumptive close...

"Sean, that's great, the team will really benefit from that. You'll get your turn to benefit when your colleagues are mystery shopped and you get to see their plans. Anyway, I guess you're OK about sharing the film with them, too?"

Sean. Yeah, why not? OK.

NDK. Great stuff, thanks Sean.

That's the sale clinched. It only really becomes an issue during the first few mystery shops; once you've had a few your team members will be fine with it. Unless it's appalling, of course. Sometimes the coachee will be devastated by what he or she has seen on film – it does happen occasionally, even with the maximum amount of ego-strengthening activity. If that's the case, our guidance to you is not to push it and accept the action plan as a fall-back position. Having said that, it is very, very rare that a coachee refuses to share the film with colleagues. Most people are fine about it.

Martin. How often does that happen in practice?

NDK. Well, let me give you an example. I worked with a well-known automotive manufacturer when we first started doing this and I trained a group of area managers. I met up with one of them about a year later when he came along for a refresher course. Someone in the group asked exactly the same question you've just asked, Martin. The area manager interrupted and said that he had conducted 47 coaching sessions using visual and telephone mystery shopping materials and in 46 of those cases the coachees had been absolutely fine about sharing the film.

The information I've received over the years is that that sort of ratio is about normal. If you do your job well, coach sensitively and with maximum ego-strengthening around the *continue to's*, you'll get excellent results and most people will agree to share their film.

37

practice time

NDK. It's time to practise. Whether you're coaching from observed behaviour, or if you're fortunate enough to have some visual or telephone mystery shopping material to refer to, the same principles apply. We're going to use the techniques and skills you have learnt today to create a commitment from your coachee to continue to do some things well, and to begin to do some things differently. And you're going to commit to support your coachee in his or her endeavours to achieve these ambitions. Practice is important because knowing what to do is not the same as...

Several. Doing what you know.

NDK. Good. A is going to coach B and C is going to observe. C will then coach A on how well she coached B. On both occasions the coach will help the coachee to develop an action plan. Guess in what form the action plan will be?

Several. Continue & Begin.

NDK. Correct. So, you'll very quickly go through the coaching process. I'm going to show you a piece of film and we're going to use that film as the resource. You can decide amongst yourselves whether the coach has just observed the coachee in action, or you have both just reviewed a mystery shopping film. It doesn't matter which because the same coaching rules apply. At the end of the coaching session the action plan will contain a number of *continue to's* and small number of *begin to's*. It might not be six and three, it might be four and two, or two and one; it doesn't really matter as long as you've been through the process. Got it?

(Nods from delegates.)

NDK. Ladies and gentlemen, before you start, let me bring your attention to this. One of the easiest things to remember, *(refers to flipchart drawing)* in addition to the model you've learnt today, is this 80/20 rule. What happens sometimes as a coach is that we get sucked into jabber, jabber, jabber, bunny, bunny, bunny, rabbit, rabbit, rabbit, rabbit. We talk too much!

What I'd like you to recognise is that the coachee should be doing 80% of the chat, with you as coach just stimulating his or her thinking with around 20% of the talking. Remember it's the coachee's plan, not yours. Coaching is about helping the coachee find his or her own solutions. If you're steering the coachee towards something with advice, those will be your solutions, and that's something else altogether called 'mentoring'. We're helping your coachee to steer his or her own course – it's much more powerful when people make their own commitments, far more powerful than complying with instructions, or 'advice'. Bear that in mind as you're conducting these *practice* sessions.

And I want you to make massive cock-ups please! The bigger the foul-up the better! Let's find out who can screw up the most, because that will be the person who learns most, and benefits most, from this practice session.

Remember, it's a simple model:

"Well, what did you think?"
"What were you pleased with?"
"What would you like to do differently next time?"
"Are you serious about this, or just messing about?"

Let's do it.

(Practise activities and reflective discussions post-activity.)

38

one-to-many coaching

NDK. Let's move on. By the way, I know what you're thinking, Daisy.

Daisy. Do you? Really? What's that?

NDK. "Why do we want to encourage the sharing of action plans?"

Daisy. Oh, yes, that's definitely what I was thinking.

(Laughter.)

NDK. Good, because this is why… when we coach someone using the Continue & Begin coaching model, either through observed behaviour, or by using mystery shopping materials, we get an enormous personal shift in awareness and behaviour from the coachee. But it's not a great return on our time investment, really.

What happens is, we get what I call *narrow and deep* performance shifts; that is, big changes in one person's behaviour. That's great for the coached employee but it does little for his or her colleagues. So what we want is to combine the *narrow and deep* coaching benefit with a *shallow and wide* approach.

That's why the sales pitch is so important at the end of the coaching session, whether you've been using mystery shopping materials, or just referring to observed behaviour. We want the coachee to agree to share his or her learning and plan of action with his or her colleagues, so that the wider team can benefit from the learning process. We can't enforce this, it's a sensitive matter, and the coachee must feel comfortable about sharing. Your coaching has to be spot on in terms of perceived benefit for the coachee, and positive enough for the coachee to feel that he or she has something to be proud of.

We call this the One-to-Many coaching session and, done well, it can reap enormous rewards for your team, for your organisation, and most importantly, for your customers.

Probably the best way to describe this is to tell you about the most impressive example of One-to-Many sessions I've experienced. It happened some years ago in a car dealership in Hertfordshire. I had trained the sales manager, Tim, in Continue & Begin and he had bravely asked if I would come along and sit in on his planned One-to-Many session. It was the first such event he'd arranged and it was in the early days when I was still fine tuning Continue & Begin. Naturally, I was delighted to attend, and strangely nervous too, even though I was just an observer.

The session took place in a conference room above the showroom at 6 p.m. In the room were the dealer principal, the sales manager and some of his team of sales executives.

One of the sales execs, Robin, had been recently featured on a mystery shopping film and had then been coached by Tim. Robin had copies of his Continue & Begin action plan with him, and a set of blank action plans.

As we sat around the conference table before kick-off, we chatted away, and then the door opened and in came two more sales execs with a stack of pizzas and a case of beer! There was a definite party atmosphere in the room.

As the sales execs tucked into their pizzas and swigged on their bottles of Bud, Tim started the session:

Tim said, "Good evening everybody. Thanks for coming along to review the Quarter 3 mystery shop. Robin was featured this quarter and we've had a good coaching session to review the film and develop Robin's action plan. Robin, can you take us through your plan, please?"

Robin said, "Sure. Here's a copy of my action plan, fellers." (It was an all male team.) "What you'll notice," he said, "is that the six *continue to's* include a fair bit around meet and greet. I'm pretty pleased with my approach, with my introduction and with my body language; I think I do a good job on those fronts. I'm also pleased with my static demo. Unfortunately the customer didn't have time for a test drive. Where I've identified some *begin to's* is in asking more qualification questions, active listening, and matching features and benefits to the customer's requirements. I know it's basic, but I've got some work to do on those areas. When you see the film, you'll get what I mean. I missed a really obvious comment by the customer that I didn't pick up on at the time. Overall, I'm reasonably pleased, but I'm disappointed I didn't ask more questions. Have a look at the film and see what you think."

At this point Robin handed out blank copies of the Continue & Begin action plan to his colleagues and turned on the DVD player. He and his colleagues watched and listened intently to the 25-minute film. As they did so, I noticed most of the sales execs making notes on their action plans.

At the end of the film, Tim said, "Thanks Robin. OK fellers, what did you think?" The sales team continued to munch on their pizzas and drink their beers, but there was a more intense feel about proceedings. A discussion began, with comments about the film and Robin's action plan. What I noticed was that each of the sales execs seemed respectful of Robin's performance and his plan. I commented on this to Tim later on. He said, "There is respect for the featured person, because they all know it could be them next, either reviewing a mystery shop film, or just working on an observed behaviour coaching session that they've had with me."

What was really powerful though, was the way that each sales exec created his own mini action plan in a diluted format, with just a couple of *continue to's* and maybe one *begin to*, from watching the film and listening to Robin.

Tim said, "As they're watching the film and listening to the coachee report on his action plan they're all thinking that they do the same, or maybe they don't do a particular skill as well as the coachee. They create their own shortened action plans based on what they've learnt from the coachee. It's a powerful peer pressure tool."

Since then I've sat in on many equally powerful One-to-Many coaching sessions, but I guess I was excited because that was the first time I'd seen it done so well, just as Tim and I had planned it. It gave me a massive buzz to see Continue & Begin being delivered so well. You can do the same in your businesses. Are you up for it?

Several. Yes! Definitely!

NDK. Good. Best go and do it then, folks.

39

embedding
your learning

NDK. We're at the end of our time together today, ladies and gentlemen. You have been a delightful group to work with. Thank you for your energy and application. I'd like to leave you with a reminder of the key learning points from today.

We have covered a lot of ground today, haven't we?

(Nods and smiles.)

NDK. Here goes...
The difference between training, mentoring and coaching,
The Model of Excellence,
Pockets of excellence,
Vast acres of mediocrity,
Pits of despair,
Explicit standards,
Consistency,
Sustainability,

Attributes of a great coach,
Coaching using observed behaviour,
Coaching using mystery shopping materials,
Judgement and observation,
Mars Bar praise,
Martin's physics A level coursework and the Structure of
    Well-Done-Ness,
Nuj's dreadful drawing of a townhouse *(laughter)*,
Good and less good,
Motivation and KITA movement,
Do or no do, no 'try',
Knowing what to do, or doing what you know?
Incidentally, and by the way,
Behaviour breeds behaviour,
PLOMs,
ICBAs,
Ah-Buts
Mood Hoovers,
20/20s,
Bus Drivers and Passengers
EGGs – what do you want to be?

Several. EGGs!

NDK. Good. And then there was...
    Continue & Begin,
    Twice as many *continues* as *begins*,
    Language that hinders,
    But Monsters,
    Shoulding all over people,

Mustabating,
If I were you – well you're not, so shut up,
Language that helps,
Well, what did you think?
Self-flagellation,
What were you really pleased with?
There must have been something?
What else?
'Yes' sets,
An occasional car salesman from Godalming,
What would you do differently?
Can't to Can,
Linguistic Cul-de-Sacs,
Thinking No-Through-Roads,
Why can't you?
Filing cabinets in the mind,
I can't because…
Freedom questions,
What would happen if you could?
What would have to happen to make that happen?
When specifically?
Are you serious about this or just messing about?
Team coaching.
Phew! Quite a lot of learning, in fact.

(Smiles and clapping.)

NDK. Now, when you go to sleep tonight, there may be one or two things whizzing around in your brain.

(Nods and smiles.)

NDK. Let me help you. Make yourself comfortable folks... put your feet flat on the floor... place your hands palms down on your laps and... take a deep breath and exhale... that's right... just relax for a spell... because... when you go to sleep tonight... just like every night... you will experience that lovely phase of sleep... where you are just starting to... drift off...

This is known as the hypnogogic phase of sleep... when you're just starting to... go to sleep. It's when you get those little twitches... as your muscles relax... and you drift off into a lovely slumber. And sometimes it's a long sleep and sometimes... like now... it can be just for a few moments... you know what it feels like, don't you? And you may be curious... to know... that during the night you almost wake up several times... as you experience what's called REM sleep. And you know what that is, don't you?

Several *(quiet mumbles)*. Rapid eye movement.

NDK. That's right. And tonight, as you sleep through the REM phases... your brain can process all the events of the day... all the things you've heard... all the things you've seen... you've felt,

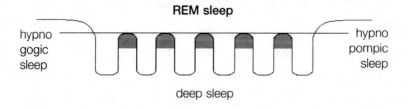

externally and internally... all the things you've smelt... and some smells were nice... and some were *less nice.*

(Smiles and gentle laughter.)

NDK. And as you process all this information from today... some now and some tonight... as you enjoy a refreshing sleep... it is becoming embedded in... your unconscious... mind. And you will file these new pieces of knowledge in the filing cabinets of your brain... ready to access them any time you need to... and by the way... while you're there, make sure to empty the 'I can't' file into the bin... or better still put the all those disempowering contents through the shredder. Because you don't need them any more...

And know that everything good you've learnt today... is now embedded in your mind... and can be used at any appropriate moment... for your benefit and for the benefit of your coachees... and as you begin to wake up... now, and in the morning... it can be a lovely dozy feeling... this is known as the hypnopompic phase of...waking up... when you have those dreams... and you can remember... just as you wake up, now... the useful information in the dreams...wide awake and alert... now... stretch... that's right... fully refreshed... feeling good... for a very good reason.

And are you ready for one final question?

(Nods from delegates.)

five little dickie birds

Five little dickie birds are sitting on a tree... two decide to fly away. How many are left? This is a very simple calculation.

5 Little Dickie Birds

Siobhan. Three.

NDK. No. Five. Two decided to fly away but they didn't take any action. The same applies to you folks. Either today has been just a fun day with some interesting ideas, or it has been a stimulus for you to take action using the skills you have learned. Which is it? Interest or action?

Several. Action!

NDK. Oh, yeah? Are you serious, or are you just messing about?

(Laughter.)

Go home, hug your friends and family, and remember today. Goodbye.

You can find out more about Nick Drake-Knight at www.ndk-group.com or email to nick@ndk-group.com.

© Nick Drake-Knight 2007

appendix a

Judgement or Observation Answers

Q1

I was watching you for some time with that customer – you did not pay attention to her.

A. Although the coach says, "I was watching you…" there is no objective statement of what specifically the coachee was doing, or not doing, that would support the supposition that "…you did not pay attention to her."

As a rule of thumb, if you can get into an argument about the statement, it is almost certainly a judgement. How do you define 'paying attention'?

A good marker is to consider whether a contradictory argument could be made from this statement, that is semantically well formed in English.

"Yes, I *was* paying attention to her!" fits as an English expression that is well formed semantically and fits the circumstances of the event.

At a more basic level of argument, if you can logically apply the confrontational question, "Oh yeah? Says who?" you have a judgement.

This example is a judgemental statement by the coach.

Q2

I saw you talking to that new member of staff about refunds and you weren't very friendly.

A. As above. The coach mind-reads the coachee and decides that he or she wasn't being friendly. What *specifically* was it the coachee did, or didn't do, that equates to "...you weren't very friendly." This is judgemental.

Q3

When you were using the computer, you stayed focused on the task. You didn't look up and make eye contact with the customer, who was a metre away from you.

A. There is a specific observation here, "You didn't look up and make eye contact with the customer, who was four feet away from you." This is specific and is an observation. There is no judgement involved in making the statement. It is fact. If the coaching process is supported by film as part of a visual mystery shopping film, the footage can be checked to verify this statement. An observation.

Q4

You did a good job with that demonstration.

A. A lovely tasty chocolate bar full of sugar. This is Mars Bar praise at its most unspecified! There are no specific reference points to this statement and, although it's a positive message, there is nothing for the coachee to take away that can used as a reference point for future excellent performance. What specifically was it that made the demonstration 'good'?

A judgement.

Q5

When the customer asked you about tariffs, you smiled at him, put down your paperwork and walked with him to the display.
A. There are three explicit observations here.

Q6

You didn't make eye contact with that customer when she asked you about the choice of fabric.
A. This is a tricky one. On the face of it this seems to be a clear-cut observation, "You didn't make eye contact…" If there was no eye contact at all, this is an accurate observation. But what if there was only a small amount of eye contact? What is the appropriate amount of eye contact? Statements about eye contact have the potential to result in dispute, even when visual mystery shopping is available for reference. A qualified 'observation'.

Q7

You handled that complaint really well.
A. More sugar-loaded chocolate. A judgement.

Q8

When the customer asked you about finance you didn't maintain eye contact. There was an opportunity to up-sell and you answered with a single word.
A. There's that ambiguity about eye contact again. The second

sentence includes a judgement and an observation. "There was an opportunity to up-sell..." is a judgement. Who says there was an opportunity? "...you answered with a single word," is a statement.

Q9

You asked four questions to find out what the customer really needed and then left the customer for about five minutes while she decided on the colour. When you came back to check on the customer you asked if she had made a decision and then you suggested a link-sale item.

A. A sequence of observations:

"You asked four questions about what the customer really needed..." Observation

"... and then left the customer for about five minutes..." Observation (Accuracy depending on the definition of 'about five minutes'.)

"You asked if she had made a decision..." Observation

"...and then you suggested a link-sale item." Observation

Q10

Who says there have to be 10 questions?